Introduction to Bible Doctrine

A Systematic Study of Seven Doctrines of the Christian Faith—*Made Easy*

"The entrance of your words gives light."
–Psalm 119:130

Introduction to Bible Doctrine

A Systematic Study of Seven Doctrines of the Christian Faith—*Made Easy*

Dr. S. Walker

Judah Publications
Orlando, FL

Introduction to Bible Doctrine

ISBN 0-9724220-0-5

Published by:
Judah Publications
P. O. Box 608505
Orlando, FL 32860
www.judahpublications.com

Printed in the United States of America

Cover Design: Octavo Design & Production

Cover Photo: Dr. S. Walker

Volume 1: Introduction to Bible Doctrine
A Systematic Study of Seven Doctrines of the Christian Faith—Made Easy
Volume 2: Introduction to Bible Origin
A Study of the Formation of the Bible
Volume 3: Introduction to Typology and Symbolism
An Expository Study of Types and Symbols Found in the Bible

Table of Contents

Introduction to Bible Doctrine outlines seven doctrines that are fundamental beliefs of Christianity. Using the "systematic" approach, these doctrines will give clearer understanding of God, Christ, The Holy Spirit, the nature of sin and God's plan of redemption as well as the provision of His Word . . . the Scriptures.

Written using modified terminology; each doctrine provides additional study helps and Scripture (which is the basis of truth for this study). A summary and questions for application of the text is also provided. ***Introduction to Bible Doctrine*** is guaranteed to strengthen your testimony of the Lord Jesus Christ, increase your spirituality and satisfy your desire for more Biblical knowledge.

"The entrance of your words gives light."
Psalm 119:130

Bible Doctrine

The definition of doctrine is ***teaching*** or ***instruction***. Doctrine is also called ***theology***, which means discourse about God. These terms are sciences that deal primarily with the knowledge of God and God's relationship with man.

False doctrine is due partly to the lack of biblical knowledge and the veracity of it. Yet, becoming knowledgeable of the doctrines of the Bible will provide a safety net against error. The knowledge of doctrinal truths will also provide a balance to beliefs and strengthen one's faith. It can contribute to the zeal of witnessing and propagation of God's Word.

There are several classifications of theological study. They are:

***Exegetical Theology*:**
Searching for and deriving at what is said to be the truth and actual meaning of the Scriptures. Hebrew and Greek are necessary for effective application.

***Dogmatic Theology*:**
Dogma is the use of selected Scriptures that help to formulate different church creeds and beliefs.

***Historical Theology*:**
The history of the church and how the Scriptures were interpreted makes use of this science.

***Biblical Theology*:**
The process of tracing each book of the Bible.

***Systematic Theology*:**
Studying biblical facts in an arranged order, which pertains to a specific subject, is a more precise method.

Introduction to Bible Doctrine provides a systematic approach giving supporting Scriptures and references with main topics. This systematic study of the doctrines of the Christian faith is intended to:

- Introduce a theological study without placing emphasis on dogma.
- Correlate truth with faith and religion to provide a firm foundation for Christian beliefs that are derived from the unchangeable Word of God.
- Provoke further study of the Word of God for Christian maturity, stability and to regress the infusion of doctrinal error.

Ephesians 4:14a "As a result, we are no longer to be children tossed here and there by waves, and carried about by every wind of doctrine."

THEOLOGY: THE DOCTRINE OF GOD

Does the Bible prove that God exists? The answer is no, the Bible does not prove the existence of God. What the Bible provides is an "affirmation" of God's existence.

Proof of God's existence is seen in creation. Other significant proofs are:

Cosmological

The universe is the *effect* of a *cause*. That is, it had to have had a cause or creator because it is a result of a source.

Teleological

The design of the universe is proof of God's existence because it systematically fulfills its purpose.

Anthropological

Human nature is also proof. No matter where he is in the world, regardless of his economical or social environment, man's nature leads him to worship a creator.

Historical

History records the involvement of God in the affairs of man giving further proof of His existence.

Common Consent

Man is compelled to worship a superior being because he feels that his destiny is controlled. This provides universal proof of the existence of God.

Many may assert that God does not exist. Those that do, have the burden of proof of the non-existence of God. To do this, one would have to be omnipotent, omnipresent and eternal. No human can put himself in God's place; therefore he cannot actually prove that God does not exist. The Atheist, who denies and does not believe in the existence of God, has this burden. [1]

THE NAMES OF GOD

Names and titles help to identify and relate to a person.

Genesis 1:1

Read Genesis Chapter One for the History of Creation.

Genesis 1:3

Genesis 1:26

Man did not evolve he was created. Matthew 19:4; Mark 10:6

Psalm 53:1
Psalm 10:4

[1] ***Dogmatic Atheist*** denies the existence of God.

Critical Atheist believes that there is no real proof of God's existence.

Skeptical Atheist doubts the ability of the human mind to know if there is a God.

Practical Atheist believes only when it is convenient.

Knowing the names by which God is called becomes helpful in fostering a closer relationship with Him. God is called:

Jehovah—Translated "LORD" in our vision. He is the eternal 'I AM.' He is "the self-existent One" who reveals Himself. 2

Exodus 3:13–14 "Then Moses said to God, 'behold, I am going to the sons of Israel, and I shall say to them, The God of your fathers has sent me to you.' Now they may say to me, 'What is His name? What shall I say to them?' and God said to Moses, 'I AM WHO I AM;' and He said, 'Thus you shall say to the sons of Israel, I AM has sent me to you.'"

2a "Yahweh"—The name God called Himself is not to be used by anyone else. Because of its sacred meaning, Jehovah was transferred to the Hebrew "Yhwh." With the use of vowels, the name Adoni (My Lord) was used instead.

2b To His own, God is called Jehovah. When involved with Gentiles, He is referred to as "God."

Compound use of the name Jehovah

Jehovah-ropheka "God that heals."

Exodus 15:26 "And He said, 'If you will give earnest heed to the voice of the LORD your God, and do what is right in His sight, and give ear to His commandments, and keep all His statutes, I will put none of the diseases on you which I have put on the Egyptians; for I, the LORD, am your healer.'"

Jehovah-meqaddeshkem "God who sanctifies."

Exodus 31:13 "But as for you, speak to the sons of Israel, saying 'You shall surely observe My sabbaths; for this is a sign between Me and you throughout your generations, that you may know that I am the LORD who sanctifies you.'"

Jehovah-tsabaoth "The LORD of the Hosts."

1st Samuel 1:3 "Now this man would go up from his city yearly to worship and to sacrifice to the LORD of hosts in Shiloh. And the two sons of Eli, Hophni and Phinehas were priests to the LORD there."

Jehovah-El Elyon "The LORD Most High."

Psalm 7:17 "I will give thanks to the LORD according to His righteousness, And will sing praise to the name of the LORD Most High."

Jehovah-roi "The LORD is My Shepherd."

Psalm 23:1 "The LORD is my Shepherd, I shall not want."

Jehovah-Jireh "The LORD will Provide."

Genesis 22:14 "And Abraham called the name of the place The LORD Will Provide, as it is said to this day, 'In the mount of the LORD it will be provided.'"

Jehovah-Nissi "The LORD is my Banner."

Exodus 17:15 "And Moses built an altar, and named it The LORD is My Banner."

Jehovah-Shalom "The LORD is my Peace."

Judges 6:24 "Then Gideon built an altar there to the LORD and named it The LORD is Peace. To this day it is still in Ophrah of the Abiezrites."

Jehovah-Shammah "The LORD is There."

Ezekiel 48:35 "The city shall be 18,000 cubits round about; and the name of the city from that day shall be, The LORD is there."

Jehovah-Tsidkenu "The LORD is our Righteousness."

Jeremiah 23:6 "In His days Judah will be saved, and Israel will dwell securely; And this is His name by which He will be called, 'The LORD our righteousness.'"

Compound use of "El" [3]

[3] "El" is used to depict the power and authority of God.

Elohim—Translated "God," is used wherever creative power or the omnipotence of God is described or implied.

Genesis 1:1 "In the beginning God created the heavens and the earth."

El Elyon—"The Most High God" the God who is exalted above that which is called god.

Genesis 14:18–20 "And Melchizedek, King of Salem brought out bread and wine; now he was a priest of God Most High. And he blessed him and said, 'Blessed be Abraham of God Most High, Possessor of heaven and earth; And blessed be God Most High, Who has delivered your enemies into your hand.' And he gave him a tenth of all."

El Shaddi (Almighty God)—signifying the "Strong One." It means "The God who is sufficient for the needs of His people." God is "El Shaddi" the breasted one, who nourishes, gives strength and satisfies His people. [4]

Genesis 17:1 "Now when Abram was ninety-nine years old, the LORD appeared to Abram and said to him, 'I am God Almighty; Walk before Me and be blameless.'"

Isaiah 28:9

[4] Shaddi derives from the word "shad," which means a breast.

El Bethel—"God of the house of God"

Genesis 31:13 "I am the God of Bethel, where you anointed a pillar, where you made a vow to Me; now arise, leave this land, and return to the land of your birth."

Genesis 35:7

El Roi—"God Sees"

Genesis 16:13 "Then she called the name of the LORD who spoke to her, 'Thou art a God who sees'; for she said 'Have I even remained alive here after seeing Him?'"

More Names of God. . .

Adoni—"Lord or Master." It conveys the idea of rulership and dominion.

Genesis 15:2 "And Abram said, 'O Lord GOD, what wilt thou give me, since I am childless, and the heir of my house is Eliezer of Damascus?'"

Ezekiel 18:4

Father—this name describes God as the producer of all things and creator of man. Therefore, all human souls are called God's offspring.

Acts 17:28 "For in Him we live and move and exist, as even some of your own poets have said, 'For we also are His offspring.'"

The Attributes of God

We've learned about the names of God, now let's define the attributes of God which will also help in relating to Him.

God is Spirit

John 4:24 "God is Spirit, and those who worship Him must worship Him in spirit and truth."

Numbers 16:22
Psalm 139:7

God is Infinite

He is God and is therefore not subject to the limitations of space and time as are humans.

2nd Chronicles 2:6
Psalm 103:19
Isaiah 57:15
Ephesians 1:23

1st Kings 8:27 "But will God indeed dwell on the earth? Behold, heaven and the highest heaven cannot contain Thee, how much less this house which I have built!"

Exodus 15:18 "The LORD shall reign forever and ever."

God is One

John 10:30

Unity in plurality, three divine personalities in absolute unity.

Deuteronomy 6:4 "Hear, O Israel! The LORD is our God, the LORD is one!"

God is Light

1st John 1:5 "And this is the message we have heard from Him and announce to you, that God is light, and in Him there is no darkness at all."

God is a consuming Fire

Hebrews 12:29 "For our God is a consuming fire."

God is Omnipotent (all-powerful)

Genesis 18:14 "Is anything too difficult for the LORD? At the appointed time I will return to you, at this time next year, and Sarah shall have a son."

Matthew 19:26
Luke 1:37
Revelation 19:6

God is Omnipresent [5]

Genesis 28:16 "Then Jacob awoke from his sleep and said, 'Surely the LORD is in this place, and I did not know it.'"

[5] God is everywhere but He does not dwell everywhere.

1st Kings 8:27
Psalm 139:7–10
Acts 17:24

God is Omniscient [6]

1st John 3:20 "In whatever our heart condemns us; for God is greater than our heart, and knows all things."

[6] God is all knowing.

Psalm 104:24
Psalm 136:5
Ephesians 3:10

God is Wise

Proverbs 3:19 "The LORD by wisdom founded the earth."

God is Sovereign [7]

Daniel 4:35 "And all the inhabitants of the earth are accounted as nothing, But He does according to His will in the host of heaven and among the inhabitants of earth; and no one can ward off His hand or say to

[7] God has absolute rights and ownership over His creations.

2nd Corinthians 6:18
Romans 9:20
Isaiah 45:9

Him, 'What hast Thou done?'"

God is the Creator

Genesis 1:1 "In the beginning God created the heavens and the earth."

God Wills

Romans 9:19 "You will say to me then, Why does He still find fault? For who resists His will?"

God is Holy

Exodus 15:11 "Who is like Thee among the gods, O LORD? Who is like thee, majestic in holiness, awesome in praises, working wonders?"

God is Righteous [8]

Genesis 18:25 "Far be it from Thee to do such a thing, to slay the righteous with the wicked, so that the righteous and the wicked are treated alike. Far be it from Thee! Shall not the Judge of all the earth deal justly?"

God is Faithful

Deuteronomy 4:31 "For the LORD your God is a compassionate God; He will not fail you nor destroy you nor forget the covenant with your fathers which He swore to them."

God is Merciful [9]

Psalm 103:8 "The LORD is compassionate and gracious, slow to anger and abounding in loving kindness."

God is Caring

1st Peter 5:6–7 "Humble yourselves, therefore, under the mighty hand of God, that He may exalt you at the proper time, casting all your anxiety upon Him, because He cares for you."

God is Love [10]

Ephesians 2:4–5 "But God, being rich in mercy, because of His great love with which He loved us, even when we were dead in our transgressions, made us alive together with Christ (by grace you have been saved)."

God is Good

Isaiah 45:18

Psalm 135:6
Romans 11:34

Exodus 3:5
Leviticus 19:2
1st Peter 1:15
Revelation 4:8

[8] God is trustworthy. Numbers 28:19

Deuteronomy 32:4
Ezra 9:15
Psalm 50:6
1st John 2:1
Revelation 16:5

Psalm 36:5
Lamentations 3:23
1st Corinthians 1:9
1st Thessalonians 5:24

[9] God is sympathetic towards His creatures.

Genesis 18:26
Exodus 34:6
Psalm 25:6
Luke 1:50

[10] Love is God's highest attribute.

Psalm 42:8
John 3:16
John 16:27
1st John 3:1

Psalm 25:8 "Good and upright is the LORD; Therefore He instructs sinners in the way."

Psalm 118:29
Matthew 7:11

God is Immutable [11]

Malachi 3:6 "For I, the LORD, do not change; therefore you, O sons of Jacob, are not consumed."

[11] God is unchangeable. "I am Yahweh: I change not." Malachi 3:6

We must always consider the differences between the names of God and the attributes of God. The names of God express God's whole being, while the attributes of God show the various sides of His nature.

FALSE VIEWS OF GOD

Agnosticism denies the human ability to know God.

Polytheism is the worship of many gods.

Pantheism identifies God as being part of the universe and not its creator.

Materialism is the belief that there is no good or evil. Because man does not possess a higher nature, what he does is based upon all that he is. Being a creature (animal), he is not responsible for his actions.

Deism teaches that God created the world and left it to be governed by natural law. ❖

Romans 1:25

NOTES

NOTES

ANGELOLOGY: THE DOCTRINE OF ANGELS

Angels are celestial creatures that were created by God. As creatures, angels refuse worship and are not to be worshipped by man.

Genesis 2:1
Nehemiah 9:6
Colossians 1:16; 2:18
Psalm 148:2

Revelation 19:10 "And I fell at his feet to worship him. And he said to me 'Do not do that; I am a fellow servant of yours and your brethren who hold the testimony of Jesus; worship God. For the testimony of Jesus is the spirit of prophecy.'"

THE CHARACTERISTICS OF ANGELS

Angels are:

Spirits—they are not limited to space, physical or natural conditions as are men. However, they have the power to become visible to be seen by men.

Psalm 104:4
Hebrews 1:14

Theophany is taken from two Greek words—"Theos" which means "God" and "Phaneroo" which means "appearance."

The "Angel of the Lord" in the Old Testament is a Theophany, the appearance of God in angelic form that is distinguished from Jehovah.

Genesis 16:7–14; 31:11
Exodus 3:2–5
1st Kings 19:5–7

Genesis 19:1–3 "Now the two angels came to Sodom in the evening as Lot was sitting in the gate of Sodom. When Lot saw them, he rose to meet them and bowed down with his face to the ground. And he said, 'Now behold, my lords, please turn aside into your servant's house, and spend the night, and wash your feet; then you may rise early and go on your way.' They said however, 'No, but we will spend the night in the square.' Yet he urged them strongly, so they turned aside to him and entered his house; and he prepared a feast for them, and baked unleavened bread, and they ate."

Masculine [12]

Mark 16:5–6 "And entering the tomb, they saw a young man sitting at the right, wearing a white robe; and they were amazed. And he said to them. "Do not be amazed you are looking for Jesus the Nazarene, who has been crucified. He has risen; He is not here; behold, here is the place where they laid Him.'"

[12] Angels are sexless and do not marry. Matthew 22:30

Immortal [13]

Hebrews 2:9 "But we do see Him who has been made for a little while lower than the angels, namely, Jesus, because of the suffering of death crowned with glory and honor, that by the grace of God, He might taste death for everyone."

[13] Angels are not subject to death.

Luke 20:36

Angels are by nature numerous in number

Matthew 26:53 "Or do you think that I cannot appeal to My Father, and He will at once put at My disposal more than twelve legions of angels?"

Deuteronomy 32:2
Hebrews 12:22
Jude 14

Angels have freewills

Jude 9 "But Michael the archangel, when he disputed with the devil and argued about the body of Moses, did not dare pronounce against him railing judgement, but said, 'The Lord rebuke you.'"

Isaiah 14:12–14
2nd Peter 2:4

Angels are placed around the Throne of God

Revelation 5:11 "And I looked, and I heard the voice of many angels around the throne and the living creatures and the elders; and the number of them was myriads of myriads, and thousands of thousands."

Revelation 7:11

Classification of Angels

The Scriptures lets us know that there are classifications of angels. Colossians 1:16 Ephesians 1:20–26

The Angel of the LORD [14]

Exodus 23:20–21 "Behold, I am going to send an angel before you to guard you along the way, and to bring you into the place which I have prepared. Be on your guard before him and obey his voice; do not be rebellious toward him, for he will not pardon your transgression, since My name is in him."

[14] The presence of Deity in angelic form. Exodus 32:34, 33:14

Michael, The Archangel or Chief Angel

Jude 9 "But Michael the archangel, when he disputed with the devil and argued about the body of Moses, did not dare pronounce against him a railing judgement, but said, 'The Lord rebuke you.'"

There are different orders or ranks among angels. Isaiah 6:2, 1st Thessalonians 4:16, Revelation 12:7

Gabriel, a high–ranking angel

Daniel 8:16 "And I heard the voice of a man between the banks of Ulai, and he called out and said, 'Gabriel, give this man an understanding of the vision.'"

Cherubim are angels connected to the redemptive purposes of God.

Exodus 25:22 "And there I will meet with you; and from above the mercy seat, from between the two cherubim which are upon the ark of the testimony, I will speak to you about all that I will give you in commandment for the sons of Israel."

The Seraphim—These angels are mentioned in the 6th chapter of Isaiah. 15

Isaiah 6:2 "Seraphim stood above Him each having six wings; with two he covered his face, and with two he covered his feet, and with two he flew."

15 Meaning "The Burning Ones."

The Angelic Host 16

Matthew 26:53 "Or do you think that I cannot appeal to My Father, and He will at once put at My disposal more than twelve legions of angels?"

16 These are the multitudes of angels that worship and serve God.

Luke 2:13
Hebrews 12:22

The Attributes of Angels

Angels are:

Obedient

1st Peter 3:22 "Who is at the right hand of God, having gone into heaven, after angels and authorities and powers had been subjected to Him?"

Psalm 103:20
Matthew 6:10
Luke 11:2
Jude 6

Reverent—they worship God.

Nehemiah 9:6 "Thou alone are the LORD. Thou has made the heavens, The heaven of heavens with all their host. The earth and all that is on it, The seas and all that is in them. Thou doest give life to all of them and the heavenly host bows down before Thee."

Philippians 2:9–11
Hebrews 1:6

Wise 17

2nd Samuel 14:20 "In order to change the appearance of things your servant Joab has done this thing. But my lord is wise, like the wisdom of the angel of God, to know all that is in the earth."

17 They are capable of discerning. Though their level of intelligence is superior, they are not all knowing (omniscient) as is God.

Matthew 24:36
1st Timothy 5:21

Mighty 18

Psalms 103:20 "Bless the LORD, you His angels, mighty in strength, who perform His word, obeying the voice of His word!"

18 They possess superior power to man but are not infinite in power (omnipotent) as is God.

2nd Peter 2:11

Holy

Mark 8:38 "For whoever is ashamed of Me and My words in this adulterous and sinful generation, the Son of Man will also be ashamed of him when He comes in the glory of His Father with the holy angels."

Matthew 25:31

Messengers of God

Genesis 19:1 "Now the two angels came to Sodom in the evening as Lot was sitting in the gate of Sodom. When Lot saw them, he rose to meet them and bowed down with his face to the ground."

Chosen by God

1st Timothy 5:21 "I solemnly charge you in the presence of God and of Christ Jesus and of His chosen angels, to maintain these principles without bias, doing nothing in a spirit of partiality."

Angels Bring:

Announcements

Daniel 10:9–14

Luke 1:13–14 "But the angel said to him, 'Do not be afraid, Zacharias, for your petition has been heard, and your wife Elizabeth will bear you a son, and you will give him the name John. And you will have joy and gladness, and many will rejoice at his birth.'"

Warnings [19]

Matthew 2:13 "Now when they had departed behold, an angel of the Lord appeared to Joseph in a dream, saying, 'Arise and take the child and His mother, and flee to Egypt, and remain there until I tell you; for Herod is going to search for the child to destroy Him.'"

[19] Angels as agents for God, also protect His people. Psalm 91:11, Daniel 3:28, Acts 5:19

Instruction

Matthew 28:5–7 "And the angel answered and said to the women, 'Do not be afraid; for I know that you are looking for Jesus who has been crucified. He is not here, for He has risen, just as He said. Come; see the place where He was lying. And go quickly and tell His disciples that He has risen from the dead; and behold, He is going before you into Galilee, there you will see Him; behold, I have told you.'"

Encouragement

Acts 27:23–24 "For this very night an angel of the God to whom I belong and whom I serve stood before me, saying, 'Do not be afraid, Paul; you must stand before Caesar; and behold, God has granted you all those who are sailing with you.'"

Revelation

Revelation 1:1 "The Revelation of Jesus Christ, which God gave Him to show to His bond-servants, the things which must shortly take place; and He sent and communicate it by His angel to His bond-servant, John."

Angels also:

Minister to the heirs of salvation

Hebrews 1:14 "Are they not all ministering spirits, sent out to render service for the sake of those who will inherit salvation?"

Protect

Daniel 6:22 "And God sent His angel and shut the lion's mouths, and they have not harmed me, inasmuch as I was found innocent before Him; and also toward you, O king, I have committed no crime."

Keep Watch

Psalm 91:11 "For He will give His angels charge concerning you, To guard you in all your ways."

Isaiah 63:9
Daniel 3:28

Lead and Guide

Exodus 14:19 "And the angel of God, who had been going before the camp of Israel, moved and went behind them; and the pillar of cloud moved from before them and stood behind them."

Exodus 23:20
1st Kings 19:5

Escort the Saints in death

Luke 16:22 "Now it came about that the poor man died and he was carried away by the angels to Abraham's bosom; and the rich man also died and was buried."

Make ways of deliverance

Acts 12:7 "And behold, an angel of the Lord suddenly appeared, and a light shone in the cell; and he struck Peter's side and roused him, saying, 'Get up quickly.' And his chains fell off his hands."

Division among Angels

We would quickly assume that there must be some type of division among angels—this assumption is true. There are holy angels, fallen angels and evil angels.

Isaiah 14:12–14, Ezekiel 28:6–19

Fallen Angels:

The angels we previously described, for the most part, are angels in their original state, purpose and character. However, God also created angels with a "free will" and with this "free will" some chose to follow Satan's leadership during his attempt to exalt himself above God. Satan and these angels were expelled from heaven. Those angels, are known as the angelic followers of the Devil, some of them are in hell, chained and await the great judgement.

2nd Peter 2:4

Revelation 12:7–9 "And there was a war in heaven, Michael and his angels waging war with the dragon. And the dragon and his angels waged war, and they were not strong enough, and there was no longer a place found for them in heaven. And the great dragon was thrown down, the serpent of old who is called the devil and Satan, who deceives the whole world; he was thrown down to the earth, and his angels were thrown down with him."

Jude 6 "And angels who did not keep their own domain, but abandoned their proper abode, He has kept in eternal bonds under darkness for the judgement of the great day."

Evil Angels

Matthew 25:41

Evil angels, which are in the world, are also referred to as Satan's angels, fallen angels, wicked spirits, demons, seductive spirits or unclean spirits. [20]

Ephesians 6:12 "For our struggle is not against flesh and blood, but against rulers, against the powers, against the world forces of this darkness, against the spiritual forces of wickedness in the heavenly places."

[20] These angels are also defined as principalities and powers. Ephesians 3:10, Colossians 1:6

The Powers of these angels are quite tremendous. [21]

Mark 5:2–5 "And when He had come out of the boat, immediately a man from the tombs with an unclean spirit met Him, and he had his dwelling among the tombs. And no one was able to bind him anymore, even with a chain; because he had often been bound with shackles and chains, and the chains had been torn apart by him, and the shackles broken in pieces, and no one was strong enough to subdue him. And constantly night and day, among the tombs and in the mountains, he was crying out and gashing himself with stones."

[21] They can control the bodies of men and animals. Acts 8:6–7, Mark 16:17–18

Demons

Demons are *"disembodied spirits"* and seek to enter into humans for possession of a body. They are often referred to as *"unclean spirits."* The Scriptures give evidence of demonic activity during the times of Christ and the Apostles.

Mark 16:9 "Now after He had risen early on the first day of the week, He first appeared to Mary Magdalene, from whom He had cast out seven demons."

Mark 1:27 "And they were all amazed, so that they debated among themselves, saying 'What is this; A new teaching with authority? He commands even the unclean spirits, and they obey Him.'"

Characteristically these Angels are:

Deaf Spirits

Mark 9:25 "And when Jesus saw that a crowd was rapidly gathering, He rebuked the unclean spirit, saying to it, 'You deaf and dumb spirit, I command you, come out of him and do not enter him again.'"

Dumb Spirits

Mark 9:17 "And one of the crowd answered Him, 'Teacher, I brought You my son, possessed with a spirit which makes him mute.'"

Lying Spirits

2nd Thessalonians 2:9–12

1st Kings 22:22 "And the LORD said unto him, Wherewith? And he said, 'I will go forth, and I will be a lying spirit in the mouth of all his prophets. And he said, 'Thou shalt persuade him, and prevail also: go forth, and do so.'" (King James Version)

Seducing Spirits

1st Timothy 4:1 "Now the Spirit speaketh expressly, that in the latter times some shall depart from the faith, giving heed to seducing spirits, and doctrines of devils."

Foul or Unclean Spirits

Revelation 18:2

Mark 9:25 "And when Jesus saw that a crowd was rapidly gathering, He rebuked the unclean spirit, saying to it, 'You deaf and dumb spirit, I command you, come out of him and do not enter him again.'"

Perverse Spirits

Isaiah 19:14 "The LORD has mingled a perverse spirit in her midst; And they have caused Egypt to err in all her work, As a drunken man staggers in his vomit."

A Spirit of Error

1st John 4:6 "We are from God; he who knows God listens to us; he who is not from God does not listen to us. By this we know the spirit of truth and the spirit of error."

A Spirit of Divination

Acts 16:16

Acts 8:9 "But there was a certain man called Simon, who previously practiced sorcery in the city and astonished the people of Samaria, claiming that he was someone great."

Familiar Spirits

1st Samuel 28:7 "Then Saul said to his servants, 'Seek for a woman who is a medium, that I may go to her and inquire of her.' And his servants said to him, 'Behold, there is a woman who is a medium at Endor.'"

They Inflict:

Infirmities—physically as well as mentally.

Luke 13:11 "And behold, there was a woman who for eighteen years had had a sickness caused by a spirit; and she was bent double, and could not straighten up at all."

Fear

2nd Timothy 1:7 "For God has not given us a spirit of fear, but of power and of love and of a sound mind."

Error

1st John 4:6 "We are of God. He who knows God hears us; he who is not of God does not hear us. By this we know the spirit of truth and the spirit of error."

Satan

Satan certainly is not a cute little red devil with cloven hooves, horns and a pitchfork. This picture of him derives from pagan mythology making his existence nothing but a fable. The truth of the matter is that Satan does exist and this is what the Bible teaches about him.

His Several Names

Satan [22]

1st Chronicles 21:1 "Then Satan stood up against Israel and moved David to number Israel."

[22] Meaning adversary, accuser.

Devil [23]

Genesis 3:4–5 "And the serpent said to the woman, 'You surely shall not die! For God knows that in the day you eat from it your eyes will be opened, and you will be like God, knowing good and evil.'"

[23] Meaning accuser or slander. Revelation 12:10

Beelzebub [24]

Mark 3:22 "And the scribes who came down from Jerusalem were saying, 'He is possessed by Beelzebub, and He casts out the demons by the ruler of the demons.'"

[24] Meaning Prince of Demons. Originally it meant Lord of Flies.

Lucifier

Isaiah 14:12 "How you are fallen from heaven, O Lucifer, son of the morning! How you are cut down to the ground, You who weakened the nations."

Belial

2nd Corinthians 6:15 "And what accord has Christ with Belial? Or what part has a believer with an unbeliever?"

Serpent

Revelation 12:9 "And the great dragon was thrown down, the serpent of old who is called the devil and Satan, who deceives the whole world; he was thrown down to the earth, and his angels were thrown down with him."

The Wicked One

1st John 2:14 "I have written unto you, fathers, because ye have known him that is from the beginning. I have written unto you, young men, because ye are strong, and the word of God abideth in you, and ye have overcome the wicked one." (King James Version)

Matthew 6:13

Prince (Ruler) of this World

John 12:31 "Now the judgement is upon this world; now the ruler of this world shall be cast out."

The Enemy

Matthew 13:39 "The enemy who sowed them is the devil, the harvest is the end of the age, and the reapers are the angels."

Son of Perdition

2nd Thessalonians 2:3–4 "Let no one deceive you by any means; for the Day will not come unless the falling away comes first, and the man of sin is revealed, the son of perdition, who opposes and exalts himself above all that is called God or that is worshiped, so that he sits as God in the temple of God, showing himself that he is God." (King James Version)

Adversary

1st Peter 5:8 "Be sober, be vigilant; because your adversary the devil walks about like a roaring lion, seeking whom he may devour."

Prince of the Power of the Air

Ephesians 2:2 "In which you formerly walked according to the course of this world, according to the prince of the power of the air, of the spirit that is now working in the sons of disobedience."

god of this age

2nd Corinthians 4:4 "In whose case the god of this world has blinded the minds of the unbelieving, that they might not see the light of the gospel of the glory of Christ, who is the image of God."

Dragon

Revelation 20:2 "And he laid hold of the dragon, the serpent of old, who is the devil and Satan, and bound him for a thousand years."

Angel of Light

2nd Corinthians 11:14 "And no wonder, for even Satan disguises himself as an angel of light."

Wolf

John 10:12 "But he who is a hireling and not the

shepherd, one who does not own the sheep, sees the wolf coming and leaves the sheep and flees; and the wolf catches the sheep and scatters them."

Accuser of the Brethern

Zechariah 3:1 "Then he showed me Joshua the high priest standing before the angel of the LORD, and Satan standing at his right hand to accuse him."

Job 1:6–8
Revelation 12:10

Father of Lies [25]

John 8:44 "You are of your father the devil, and you want to do the desires of your father. He was a murderer from the beginning, and does not stand in the truth, because there is no truth in him. Whenever he speaks a lie, he speaks from his own nature; for he is a liar, and the father of lies."

25 Satan is a deceiver of the truth and the creator of lies.

Genesis 3:1–4
2nd Timothy 2:26
Revelation 2:9

Roaring Lion

1st Peter 5:8 "Be of sober spirit, be on the alert. Your adversary, the devil, prowls about like a roaring lion, seeking someone to devour."

The Ruler of Darkness

Ephesians 6:12 "For our struggle is not against flesh and blood, but against the rulers, against the powers, against the world forces of this darkness, against the spiritual forces of wickedness in the heavenly places."

Murderer [26]

John 8:44a "You are of your father the devil, and you want to do the desires of your father. He was a murderer from the beginning."

26 He kills and destroys life.

Tempter

Matthew 4:3 "And the tempter came and said to Him, 'If you are the Son of God, command that these stones become bread.'"

The Origin of Satan

Satan was a created being and held the highest position of the entire Angelic Host. He was created in perfect beauty as his name "Son of the Morning" depicts. Pride and choosing his own will above the will of God was the cause of his downfall.

Ezekiel 28:14–15
Ezekiel 28:12–17
Isaiah 14:12–15

Satan's Character

Satan has Power

Job 1:9–12 "Then Satan answered the LORD, 'Does Job fear God for nothing? Hast Thou not made a hedge about him and his house and all that he has, on every side? Thou hast blessed the work of his hands, and his possessions have increased in the land. But put forth Thy hand now and touch all that he has; he will surely curse Thee to Thy face.' Then the LORD said to Satan, 'Behold, all that he has is in your power, only do not put forth your hand to him.' So Satan departed from the presence of the LORD."

Satan is Deceitful and Cunning

2nd Corinthians 11:14 "And no wonder, for even Satan disguises himself as an angel of light."

Satan is Fearful

James 4:7 "Submit therefore to God. Resist the devil and he will flee from you."

Acts 10:38

The Activity of Satan

To tempt Man

Matthew 4:1 "Then Jesus was led up by the Spirit into the wilderness to be tempted by the devil."

Luke 13:16

He is the Producer of Sickness [27]

1st Corinthians 5:5 "I have decided to deliver such a one to Satan for the destruction of his flesh, that his spirit may be saved in the day of the Lord Jesus."

27 Satan produces all types of sickness and disease (physical, mental and emotional).

He has the Power of Death [28]

Hebrews 2:14 "Since then the children share in flesh and blood, He Himself likewise also partook of the same, that through death He might render powerless him who had the power of death, that is the devil."

28 His power was demised by the resurrection of Christ. John 8:44

He also produces Temptation

Mark 1:13 "And He was in the wilderness forty days being tempted by Satan; and He was with the wild beasts, and the angels were ministering to Him."

Matthew 4:1–11
1st Corinthians 7:5
John 14:30

Satan lays Snares for Men [29]

2nd Timothy 2:26 "And they may come to their

29 Meaning traps, entrapment.

senses and escape from the snare of the devil, having been held captive by him to do his will."

He Snatches the Word of God from the hearts of men.

Matthew 13:19 "When anyone hears the Word of the kingdom, and does not understand it, the evil one comes and snatches away what has been sown in his heart. This is the one on whom seed was sown beside the road."

He Sows Tares among the People of God.

Matthew 13:38–39 "And the field is the world; and as for the good seed, these are the sons of the kingdom; and the tares are the sons of the evil one; and the enemy who sowed them is the devil, and the harvest is the end of the age; and the reapers are angels."

Satan's Limitations

John 12:31

The believer will overcome Satan and stand victorious if he adapts the following disposition: [30]

[30] Satan's best weapon is deceitfulness. Resisting his lies with the truth of God's Word is the believer's best offensive weapon.

#1 Resistance

James 4:7 "Submit therefore to God. Resist the devil and he will flee from you."

#2 Assert the power and authority that comes with Redemption.

Revelation 12:10–11 "And I heard a loud voice in heaven, saying 'Now the salvation, and the power, and the kingdom of our God and the authority of His Christ have come, for the accuser of our brethren has been thrown down, who accuses them before our God day and night. And they overcame him because of the blood of the Lamb and because of the word of their testimony, and they did not love their life even to death.'"

#3 Maintain spiritual sobriety [31]

[31] Be watchful for signs of danger and entrapment.

1st Peter 5:8 "Be of sober spirit, be on the alert. Your adversary, the devil, prowls about like a roaring lion, seeking someone to devour."

#4 Put on the Armor of God [32]

[32] The Armor of God is found in Ephesians 6:10–18

Ephesians 6:10–11 "Finally, be strong in the Lord, and in the strength of His might. Put on the full armor of God, that you may be able to stand firm against the schemes of the devil." ❖

NOTES

NOTES

Hamartiology: The Doctrine of Sin

The Origin of Sin

Lucifer, who was expelled from heaven when he chose his will over the will of God, originally brought sin into the universe.

Ezekiel 28:11–19

The introduction of sin to the human race was by Lucifer who became the Devil or Satan. The first book of the Bible, Genesis, gives the details of the fall of man.

Many assert that God must have created sin, but this simply is not true. Sin, by definition, is anything that is in contrast to the moral character of God. Man, who is created in the image and likeness of God, chooses (by way of his own will) to commit sin. Man is by no means a victim of fate or doomed by chance because he has the ability to decide between what is right and what is wrong. One perfect example is given when God warned Adam of the consequences of eating from a particular tree, which He had forbidden. Adam chose to do his own will over the expressed will of God. Therefore, the consequences that followed were based solely on his predetermination rather than fate. [33]

[33] Factors that led to sin entering the human race are found in Genesis, Chapter 3.
#1 Doubting God's grace—Genesis 3:1
#2 Adding to God's command—Genesis 3:2–3
#3 Lying—Genesis 3:4
#4 Pride—Genesis 3:5

There are three realms of sin:

#1 Sin is an action

#2 Sin can be a state or condition that a person is in

John 8:11

#3 Man is sinful by nature

Romans 3:23

God created man with a free will. Yet, knowing that man would use his own will in some cases against the will of his creator, God had a plan to save man from his own destruction. Demonstrating His love for mankind, God's perfect plan was Jesus Christ.

Ephesians 2:4–8 "But God, being rich in mercy, because of His great love with which He loved us, even when we were dead in our transgressions, made us alive together with Christ (by grace you have been saved), and raised us up with Him, and seated us with Him in the heavenly places, in Christ Jesus, in order that in the ages to come He might show the surpassing riches of His grace in kindness toward us in Christ Jesus. For by grace you have been saved through faith; and that not of yourselves, it is the gift of God."

SIN IS REALIZED BY:

Scripture

Galatians 3:22 "But the Scripture hath concluded all under sin, that the promise by faith of Jesus Christ might be given to them that believe." (King James Version)

Creation

Genesis 3:17 "Then to Adam He said, 'Because you have listened to the voice of your wife, and have eaten from the tree about which I commanded you saying, 'You shall not eat from it'; Cursed is the ground because of you; In toil you shall eat of it all the days of your life.'"

Confession [34]

Romans 5:12 "Therefore, just as through one man sin entered into the world, and death through sin, and so death spread to all men, because all sinned."

[34] Sin is Universal. Isaiah 6:5 Exodus 9:27b, Matthew 27:4

Romans 1:24–32

Society

Romans 1:18 "For the wrath of God is revealed from heaven against all ungodliness and unrighteousness of men, who suppress the truth in unrighteousness."

THE NATURE AND BIBLICAL VIEW OF SIN

Missing the Mark [35]

Romans 3:23 "For all have sinned and fall short of the glory of God."

[35] Sinners miss the divine standard of God.

Daniel 9:11

Transgression [36]

Psalm 51:1 "Be gracious to me, O God, according to thy loving kindness; According to the greatness of Thy compassion blot out my transgressions."

[36] Overstepping the divine boundary between good and evil unintentionally or intentionally.

Rebellion against God

Isaiah 1:2 "Hear, O heavens, and give ear, O earth: for the LORD hath spoken, I have nourished and brought up children, and they have rebelled against me."

Debt [37]

[37] Everyone is obligated to obey the commandments of God. To break them would mean that a debt is owed to God that would require pardon or remission, which is accomplished by Jesus Christ.

Hebrews 2:1–4 "For this reason we must pay much closer attention to what we have heard, lest we drift away from it. For if the word spoken through angels proved unalterable, and every transgression and disobedience received a just recompense, how shall we escape if we neglect so great a salvation? After it was at the first spoken through the Lord, it was confirmed to us by those who heard, God also bearing witness with them, both by signs and wonders and by various miracles and by gifts of the Holy Spirit according to His own will."

Error [38]

[38] Doing wrong because of ignorance.

Hebrews 9:7 "But into the second only the high priest enters, once a year, not without taking blood, which he offers for himself and for the sins of the people committed in ignorance."

Trespass [39]

[39] Exerting self–will above divine authority.

Ephesians 2:1 "And you were dead in your trespasses and sins."

To Fall or Fault [40]

[40] Conduct which contrasts godliness.

2nd Peter 1:10–11 "Therefore, brethren, be all the more diligent to make certain about His calling and choosing you; for as long as you practice these things, you will never stumble for in this way the entrance into the eternal kingdom of our Lord and Savior Jesus Christ will be abundantly supplied to you."

Ungodliness [41]

[41] To be without worship or reverence to God and sacred things.

Romans 1:18 "For the wrath of God is revealed from heaven against all ungodliness and unrighteousness of men, who suppress the truth in unrighteousness."

Lawlessness [42]

[42] Deliberate disregard for God's laws.

1st John 3:4 "Everyone who practices sin also practices lawlessness; and sin is lawlessness."

Unbelief

1st John 5:10

John 16:8–9 "And He, when He comes, will convict the world concerning sin and righteousness, and judgment; concerning sin, because they do not believe in Me."

The Penalty of Sin

The penalty of sin is death. Death in Scripture does not mean absolute destruction or annihilation; it is defined in three ways: Spiritual, Physical and Eternal death.

Romans 6:23 "The wages of sin is death, but the free gift of God is eternal life in Christ Jesus our Lord."

Spiritual Death [43]

1st Timothy 5:6 "But she who gives herself to wanton pleasure is dead even while she lives."

Physical Death [44]

Hebrews 9:27 "And inasmuch as it is appointed for men to die once and after this comes judgement."

Eternal Death [45]

Revelation 20:14 "Death and hell were cast into the lake of fire. This is the second death."

Other terms used to describe the penalty of sin are:

Being Lost

John 17:12 "While I was with them, I was keeping them in Thy name which Thou hast given Me; and I guarded them, and not one of them perished but the son of perdition, that the Scripture might be fulfilled."

Perdition or Destruction

Matthew 7:13 "Enter by the narrow gate; for the gate is wide, and the way is broad that leads to destruction, and many are those who enter by it."

Punishment [46]

Matthew 25:46 "And these will go away into eternal punishment, but the righteous into eternal life." ❖

[43] While living, the sinner who disobeys God deprives his spirit and experiences spiritual death.

[44] This death only effects the body. It is universal and inevitable.

Genesis 3:39

[45] Called the "Second Death," this is spiritual death that is prolonged after the death of the body. It is eternal separation from God. The sinner will be conscious of his suffering and condition.

[46] Punishment is eternal and is in contrast to chastisement (which is for the saved).

NOTES

NOTES

CHRISTOLOGY: THE DOCTRINE OF CHRIST

The question most often asked by many is "who is Christ?" The best way to answer this question is to explain the names by which Christ is known.

He is known as ***The Son of God.***

This title proclaims the Deity of Christ. Son of man means born of man, Son of God means born of God.

Mark 1:1 "The beginning of the gospel of Jesus Christ, the Son of God."

John 1:18 "No man hath seen God at any time; the only begotten Son, which is in the bosom of the Father, he hath declared him." (King James Version)

Consider that Christ at a very early age was conscious of His unique relationship with God whom He described as His Father. Later in His ministry, Christ continued to declare that He was The Son of God.

Luke 2:49 "And He said to them, 'Why is it that you were looking for Me? Did you not know that I had to be in my Father's house?'"

John 16:28 "I come forth from the Father, and have come into the world; I am leaving the world again, and going to the Father."

God Himself, at the Jordan River, declared the Deity of Christ as being His Son.

Matthew 3:17 "And behold a voice out of the heavens, saying, 'This is My beloved Son, in whom I am well pleased.'"

Peter was highly commended for his recognition of Christ as being The Son of God.

Matthew 16:16 "And Simon Peter answered and said, 'Thou art the Christ, the Son of the living God.'"

Satan, as well as demons, attested to the Deity of Christ.

Matthew 4:3 "And the tempter came and said to Him, 'If You are the Son of God, command that these stones become bread.'"

Luke 4:41a "And the demons also were coming out of many, crying out and saying, 'You are the Son of God!'"

We must be sure to clearly distinguish the difference between *a* Son of God and *the* Son of God. Jesus is not *a* Son of God in the general sense as are men and angels. He is *the* Son of God having a relationship with the Father not to be experienced by any other being. Jesus could have avoided the death of the cross, had He accepted the lesser title as *a* Son of God, thereby denying that He was *The* Son of God.

Jesus had knowledge of the evil of sin yet in His words and actions, He remained sinless.

John 8:46 "Which one of you convicts Me of sin: If I speak truth, why do you not believe Me?"

He is called ***Lord,*** which indicates: [48]

#1 *Deity*

John 13:13 "You call Me Teacher and Lord; and you are right, for so I am."

#2 *Sovereignty*

2nd Corinthians 5:15 "And that he died for all, that they which live should not henceforth live unto themselves, but unto him which died for them, and rose again." (King James Version)

Ephesians 1:22–23 "And He put all things in subjection under His feet, and gave Him as head over all things to the church, which is His body, the fullness of Him who fills all in all."

#3 *Exaltation* [49]

Acts 2:36 "Therefore let all the house of Israel know for certain that God has made Him both Lord and Christ—this Jesus whom you crucified."

He is called ***The Son of Man***

The "Son of Man" is a title Jesus gave Himself. This title connects our Lord with humanity as He relates or identifies with man's infirmities.

1st Corinthians 15:45–49 "So also it is written, 'The first man, Adam, became a living soul.' The last Adam became a life–giving spirit. However, the spiritual is not first, but the natural; then the spiritual. The first man is from the earth, earthly; the second man is from

[48] The Jews in recognition of the Deity of Christ, to whom they ascribed Lordship and rendered service, used the title "The Lord Jesus."

[49] He was exalted to Lordship over all things. Romans 10:12, Acts 10:36

heaven. As is the earthly, so also are those who are earthly; and as is the heavenly, so also are those who are heavenly. And just as we have borne the image of the earthly, we shall also bear the image of the heavenly."

Philippians 2:5–8 "Have this attitude in yourselves which was also in Christ Jesus, who, although He existed in the form of God, did not regard quality with God a thing to be grasped, but emptied Himself, taking the form of a bond–servant, and being made in the likeness of men. And being found in appearance as a man, He humbled Himself by becoming obedient to the point of death, even death on a cross."

Incarnation is one of the most arguable facts pertaining to Christ's Deity. The Son of God becoming the Son of Man with the same authority and power of God is the basis for this. Just how did Jesus, The Son of God become The Son of Man? The answer is given in the Scripture as follows:

Luke 1:26–38

Matthew 1:18–23

How:

Luke 1:30–35

The Son of Man (Christ) entered this world by being conceived of Mary by the Holy Spirit, which gives the basis for the doctrine of incarnation; God "The Son of God" became man.

John 1:14 "And the Word was made flesh, and dwelt among us, (and we beheld His glory, the glory as of the only begotten of the Father), full of grace and truth."

The incarnation of Christ does not mean that God ceased to be God by becoming a human being. The Son of God became man also . . . God incarnated.

Unity of the two natures in one person . . . Jesus Christ.

Why:

God directed the works and words spoken by Jesus. Jesus became the revealer of God through incarnation.

John 5:19 "Jesus therefore answered and was saying to them 'Truly, truly, I say to you, the Son can do nothing of Himself, unless it is something He sees the Father doing: for whatever the Father does, these things the Son also does in like manner.'"

Results [50]

The results of the incarnation are extremely beneficial to mankind. By the Son of God becoming the Son of Man, we (the children of men) become the sons of God

[50] We are transformed from earthly and fleshly existence to spiritual and heavenly existence.

in the spiritual sense.

John 1:12 "But as many as received Him, to them He gave the right to become children of God, even to those who believe in His name."

1st John 3:2 "Beloved, now are we the sons of God, and it doth not yet appear what we shall be: but we know that, when he shall appear, we shall be like him; for we shall see him as he is." (King James Version)

He is called ***The Christ*** [51]

Christ is the Greek form of the Hebrew word "Messiah" which is the official or formal name of Jesus. This title connects Him to the Old Testament foresight of the prophet, priest and king that was to come.

Jesus officially became "The Christ" when He was anointed by the Holy Spirit. It was customary that prophets, priests and kings be anointed with oil, which signified the honor of the office.

Luke 3:21–22 "Now it came about when all the people were baptized, that Jesus also was baptized, and while He was praying, heaven was opened, and the Holy Spirit descended upon Him in bodily form like a dove, and a voice came out of heaven, 'Thou are My beloved Son, in Thee I am well pleased.'"

He is called ***Emmanuel***—"God with us" [52]

Matthew 1:23 "Behold, The virgin shall be with child, and shall bear a Son, and they shall call His name Emmanuel, which translated means, 'God with us.'"

He is called ***The Son of David*** [53]

This Messianic title describes Jesus as being in direct lineage of David. The Messiah had to have been a descendent of David. This is one of the most important factors in identifying the "Messiah," since the promise of God secured the prosperity, royal authority and rule, forever, of the house of David.

Luke 1:31–33 "And behold, you will conceive in your womb, and bear a son, and you shall name Him Jesus. He will be great, and will be called the Son of the Most High; and the Lord God will give Him the throne of His father David; and He will reign over the house of Jacob forever; and His kingdom will have no end."

[51] The "official" name of Jesus.

[52] This name proves the preexistence of Christ. John 1:1

[53] The royal title of Jesus proves that He was the fulfillment of the Davidic Covenant.

He is called ***The Word*** [54]

Jesus is known as the WORD because He discloses the thoughts and expressions of eternal God.

Hebrews 1:1–3 "God, in sundry times and in diverse manners spake in the time past unto the fathers by the prophets, Hath in these last days spoken unto us by his son, whom he hath appointed heir of all things, by whom also he made the worlds; Who being the brightness of his glory, and the express image of his person, and upholding all things by the word of his power, when he had by himself purged our sins, sat down on the right hand of the Majesty on high." (King James Version)

Colossians 2:2–3 "That their hearts might be comforted, being knit together in love, and unto all riches of the full assurance of understanding, to the acknowledgement of the mystery of God, and the Father, and of Christ; in whom are hid all the treasures of wisdom and knowledge." (King James Version)

The Greek word Logos means: something said, a thought or concept. This is applied to Jesus who is the expression of God with wisdom and knowledge of Him. In past times, God spoke through prophets, visions and dreams. Christ became the more definite way that God expresses Himself. John 14:7–10

[54a] He is the Word made flesh. John 1:14–18

[54b] He is God. John 1:1

John 20:28
Romans 9:5
Titus 2:13

Alpha and Omega

Revelation 1:8 "'I am the Alpha and the Omega,' says the Lord God, 'who is and who was and who is to come, the Almighty.'"

Revelation 22:13

King of Kings

Revelation 17:14 "These will wage war against the Lamb, and the Lamb will overcome them, because He is Lord of lords and King of kings, and those who are with Him are called and chosen and faithful."

Revelation 19:16

The Truth

John 14:6 "Jesus said to him, 'I am the way, and the truth, and the life; no one comes to the Father, but through Me.'"

Lamb of God

John 1:29 "The next day he saw Jesus coming to him, and said, 'Behold, the Lamb of God who takes away the sin of the world!'"

The Way

John 14:1–6 "'Let not your heart be troubled; believe in God, believe also in Me. In My Father's house are many dwelling places; if it were not so, I would have told you; for I go to prepare a place for you. And if I go and prepare a place for you, I will come again, and receive you to Myself; that where I am, there you may be also. And you know the way where I am going.' And Thomas said to Him, 'Lord, we do not know where You are going, how do we know the way?' Jesus said to him, 'I am the way, and the truth, and the life; no one comes to the Father, but through Me.'"

The ascension of Christ was what prepared the way for the saints.

The Offices of Christ

Christ held three offices as the mediator between God and His people; these are the perfect prophet, priest and king.

Perfect Prophet [55]

Christ is the "perfect prophet" because He was not merely God's representative as was other prophets, He was God (The Son) making Him therefore "better than" the prophets.

Hebrews 1:1–2 "God who at sundry times and in diverse manners spake in time unto the fathers by the prophets, Hath in these last days spoken unto us by His Son, whom he hath appointed heir of all things, by whom also He made the worlds."

[55] Prophets were God's representatives to His people.

Perfect Priest [56]

Priests offered sacrifices to God on behalf of the people for their sins. Christ is the "perfect priest" because He himself was the sacrifice. Being raised again from the dead and seated at the right hand of God the Father, He continues to compassionately make intercession for us.

Hebrews 7:23–25 "And the former priests, on the one hand, existed in greater numbers, because they were prevented by death from continuing, but He, on the other hand, because He abides forever, holds His priesthood permanently. Hence, also, He is able to save forever those who draw near to God through Him, since He always lives to make intercession for them."

[56] Priests were the people's representatives to God. The Priest made their offerings to God with compassion on behalf of the people. Read the Book of Hebrews.

Perfect King

The official office of the prophet and king was combined and held by one person. Melchizedek typified Christ as the "king–priest." [57]

[57] Types are divine illustrations that are found in the Old Testament. Anti–types are the fulfillment of "types" and are found in the New Testament. For example: Moses is a "type" of Christ as a deliverer.

Hebrews 7:1–3 "For this Melchizedek, King of Salem, priest of the Most High God, who met Abraham as he was returning from the slaughter of the kings and blessed him, to whom also Abraham apportioned a tenth part of all the spoils, was first of all, by the translation of his name, king of righteousness, and then also King of Salem, which is king of peace. Without father, without mother, without genealogy, having neither beginning of days nor end of life, but made like the Son of God, he abides a priest perpetually."

Notice that:

1. Melchizedek was a king and priest.
2. He blessed Abraham.
3. Abraham paid tithes to him.
4. Melchizedek's name meant "King of Righteousness."
5. He was the King of Salem (meaning peace).
6. There was no record of Melchizedek's beginning or end.

Christ is the anti–type of Melchizedek. He, by descent of David, is the Messiah (the anointed king whose kingdom is of righteousness, peace, prosperity and is never ending). Hence, He is the "perfect king." He was not crowned with a crown of gold, nor does His kingdom compare to this world.

Isaiah 11:1–9

John 18:36 "Jesus answered, 'My kingdom is not of this world. If My kingdom were of this world, then My servants would be fighting, that I might not be delivered up to the Jews; but as it is, My kingdom is not of this realm.'"

John 19:2 "And the soldiers wove a crown of thorns and put it on His head, and arrayed Him in a purple robe."

The Redemptive Work of Christ

His Death [58]

Sin destroyed the relationship between God and man. It became a barrier that could not be moved by human methods. The death of Christ repaired the relationship between God and mankind because it appeased the offense of sin.

[58] The most significant work of Christ was His dying for man's sins. This work accomplished atonement for men.

Ephesians 2:14
1st John 2:2

Romans 3:24 "Being justified as a gift by His grace through the redemption which is in Christ Jesus;

whom God displayed publicly as a propitiation in His blood through faith, This was to demonstrate His righteousness, because in the forbearance of God He passed over the sins previously committed."

His Resurrection

Romans 1:4
Romans 8:34
Hebrews 13:20

Christ's claims of being a Savior, Lord and Son of God were proven by His resurrection. Being resurrected and seated on the right–hand of God the Father, He is our High Priest in heaven who is sympathetic toward us (having Himself known our sorrows and borne our infirmities). Through Him we have forgiveness of sins and peace with God.

Hebrews 4:14–15 "Since then we have a great High Priest who has passed through the heavens, Jesus the Son of God, let us hold fast our confessions. For we do not have a high priest who cannot sympathize with our weaknesses, but one who has been tempted in all things as we are, yet without sin."

His Ascension [59]

[59] All authority was given to Him in heaven and on earth. Matthew 28:18

Christ's ascension into heaven (which was witnessed by His disciples) made Him no longer a Christ after the flesh rather it made Him a heavenly Christ.

Mark 16:19
Luke 24:50–52

Acts 1:9–11 "And after He had said these things, He was lifted up while they were looking on, and a cloud received Him out of their sight. And as they were gazing intently into the sky while He was departing, behold, two men in white clothing stood beside them; and they also said, 'Men of Galilee, why do you stand looking into the sky? This Jesus, who has been taken up from you into heaven, will come in just the same way as you have watched Him go into heaven.'"

The Old Testament prediction of Christ's ascension is found in Psalm 68:18

The Continued Work of Christ

He *Abides* within the believer

John 15:11

John 15:5 "I am the vine, you are the branches; he who abides in Me, and I in him, he bears much fruit; for apart from Me you can do nothing."

He is ***Head*** of the Church

Colossians 1:18 "He is also head of the body, the church; and He is the beginning, the first–born from the dead; so that He Himself might come to have first place in everything."

He is our ***High Priest*** in heaven

Hebrews 4:14 "Since then we have a great High Priest who has passed through the heavens, Jesus the Son of God, let us hold fast our confession."

He gives ***Gifts*** to the body [60]

Ephesians 4:8 "Therefore it says 'When He ascended on high, He led captive a host of captives, and He gave gifts to men.'"

[60] These gifts are: Apostles, Prophets, Evangelist, Pastors and Teachers. Ephesians 4:11–13.

He is our ***Intercessor***

Hebrews 9:24 "For Christ did not enter a holy place made with hands, a mere copy of the true one, but into heaven itself, now to appear in the presence of God for us."

Hebrews 7:25
John 17

He sent the ***Comforter***

John 16:7 "But I tell you the truth, it is to your advantage that I go away; for if I do not go away, the Helper shall not come to you; but if I go, I will send Him to you."

He gives ***Position*** in heaven

Ephesians 2:6 "And raised us up with Him in the heavenly places, in Christ Jesus."

He gives ***Eternal Life***

John 10:28 "And I give eternal life to them, and they shall never perish; and no one shall snatch them out of My hand."

He is the ***Resurrection***

Philippians 3:21
2nd Timothy 4:1

John 11:25–26 "And Jesus said to her, 'I am the resurrection and the life; he who believes in Me shall live even if he dies. And everyone who lives and believes in Me shall never die. Do you believe this?'"

He prepares a ***Place*** in heaven

John 14:1–2 "Let not your heart be troubled; believe in God, believe also in Me. In my Father's house are many dwelling places; if it were not so, I would have told you; for I go to prepare a place for you."

THE DIVINE ATTRIBUTES OF CHRIST

Revelations 4:11

Christ and the Father are *one* and therefore have the

same attributes.

John 10:30 "I and my Father are One."

Creator

Colossians 1:15–17 "And He is the image of the invisible God, the first–born of all creation. For by Him all things were created, both in the heavens and on earth, visible and invisible, whether thrones or dominions or rulers or authorities—all things have been created by Him and for Him. And He is before all things and in Him all things hold together."

Christ is ***Omnipresent***

Matthew 28:20 "Teaching them to observe all that I commanded you; and lo, I am with you always, even to the end of the age."

He is ***Omniscient***

John 16:30 "Now we know that You know all things, and have no need for anyone to question You; by this we believe that You came from God."

He is ***Omnipotent***

Matthew 28:18 "And Jesus came up and spoke to them, saying 'All authority has been given to Me in heaven and on earth.'"

Hebrews 1:3 "And He is the radiance of His glory and the exact representation of His nature, and upholds all things by the word of His power. When He had made purification of sins, He sat down at the right hand of the Majesty on high.'" ❖

NOTES

NOTES

SOTERIOLOGY: THE DOCTRINE OF SALVATION

Salvation is primarily a "state of grace . . . a blessing." There are three aspects of salvation: *justification, regeneration,* and *sanctification.*

JUSTIFICATION [61]

Justification and righteousness are inseparable in Scripture. This aspect of salvation originates by grace. Justification is gained through the redemptive and propitiatory work of Jesus Christ.

Romans 3:24–25 "Being justified as a gift by His grace through the redemption which is in Christ Jesus; whom God displayed publicly as a propitiation in His blood through faith. This was to demonstrate His righteousness, because in the forbearance of God He passed over the sins previously committed."

A person becomes justified by means of his belief that Christ died for his sins on the cross at Calvary.

1st Corinthians 1:30

[61] To justify is to "make right," "vindicate" or "absolve."

Justification is by faith and not works.

Romans 3:28 "For we maintain that a man is justified by faith apart from works of the Law."

Galatians 2:16 "Nevertheless knowing that a man is not justified by the works of the Law but through faith in Christ Jesus, even we have believed in Christ Jesus, that we may be justified by faith in Christ, and not by the works of the Law; since by the works of the Law shall no flesh be justified."

Justification by nature is divine. It is the judicial act of God, who is the judge of sin and can justly declare the repenting sinner, who believes in Jesus Christ righteous.

Try to picture a courtroom setting. The sinner appears in court for sentencing for his sins before the righteous and just judge . . . God. His advocate or mediator, Jesus Christ, represents the sinner. The atonement is what is used to appease the crime. The sinner's repentance is accepted and pardon is granted. He is acquitted . . . he's free to live his life as though he never committed the crime. Read the 4th and 5th chapters of Romans.

The unity of justification and righteousness is very necessary to man. It puts man in right standing with God. The Gospel tells how man, who is sinful by nature, can be changed both in position and condition and be right with God.

The source of justification is grace, which is a pure benefit from God. It is a gift, unrecompensed; you cannot pay God for it. God grants grace solely by His pure kindness and unmerited favor.

Grace is a benefit from God. God deals with sinners

through grace, which is absolutely apart from merit or demerit.

Romans 6:23 "For the wages of sin is death, but the free gift of God is eternal life in Christ Jesus our Lord."

Remember also, that there was a price paid. Man's pardon was not simply excused because of the graciousness of God, but through the blood of Jesus Christ.

1st Corinthians 15:3 "For I delivered to you as of first importance what I also received, that Christ died for our sins according to the Scriptures."

God treats a sinner righteous because He Himself provided him with righteousness. Though the believing sinner did not earn the title (righteous) himself, he receives it because Christ earned it for him. He is therefore, declared righteous due to the redemptive work of Christ.

2nd Corinthians 5:21 "He made Him who knew no sin to be sin on our behalf, that we might become the righteousness of God in Him."

REGENERATION 62

The nature of regeneration is also divine. A person who is dead in trespasses and sin is in need of a new life. This new life can only be given by divine means. Regeneration gives the believer a life which is higher than the old . . . a life that is in personal union with Jesus Christ.

Ephesians 2:1–6 "And you were dead in your trespasses and sins, in which you formerly walked according to the course of this world, according to the prince of the power of the air, of the spirit that is now working in the sons of disobedience. Among them we too all formerly lived in the lusts of our flesh, indulging the desires of the flesh and of the mind and were by nature children of wrath, even as the rest. But God, being rich in mercy, because of His great love which He loved us, even when we were dead in our transgressions, made us alive together with Christ (by grace you have been saved), and raised us up with Him and seated us with Him in the heavenly places, in Christ Jesus."

The following are New Testament terms that describe

62a Regeneration in Greek means "re–creation," "make new" which refers to the "new birth" or to be "born again."

Titus 3:5

62b Being bought with a price, read 1st Corinthians 6:20

62c Saved by Grace, read Romans 3:24

regeneration as a "radical change" in an individual's life, character and desires.

A Birth [63]

John 3:5 "Jesus answered, 'Truly, truly, I say to you, unless one is born of water and the Spirit, he cannot enter into the kingdom of God.'"

[63] The believer is begotten of God, 1st John 5:1. He is born of the Spirit, John 3:8.

A Cleansing [64]

Titus 3:5 "He saved us, not on the basis of deeds which we have done in righteousness, but according to His mercy, by the washing of regeneration and renewing by the Holy Spirit."

[64] God saves us by means of the "washing of regeneration."

A Quickening [65]

Ephesians 4:23–24 "And that you be renewed in the spirit of your mind, and put on the new self, which in the likeness of God has been created in righteousness and holiness of the truth."

[65] Not only are we saved by the "washing of regeneration" but by "the renewing of the Holy Spirit." Titus 3:5, Col. 3:10

A New Creation [66]

2nd Corinthians 5:17 "Therefore if any man is in Christ, he is a new creature; the old things passed away; behold, new things have come."

[66] God, who created man and breathed the breath of life in him, creates him over again by the Holy Spirit.

The special agent in regeneration is the Holy Spirit who produces the change. Because regeneration is a divine act, man's only preparation for it is repentance and faith.

Stated boldly, regeneration is not reformation of the old nature. The new birth is a creative act of the Holy Spirit on the condition of faith in the crucified Christ. The believer becomes a partaker of Christ's divine nature and life.

John 1:12–13 "But as many as received Him, to them He gave the right to become children of God, even to those who believe in His name, who were born not of the blood, nor of the will of the flesh, nor of the will of man, but of God."

John 3:6

Sanctification

Sanctification occurs in three phases: **Positional, Progressive** and **Final.**

The *first* occurrence of sanctification is *positional.* The believer upon justification becomes sanctified. He is cleansed and becomes, so to speak, the property of God.

1st Corinthians 6:11 "And such were some of you; but you were washed, but you were sanctified, but you were justified in the name of the Lord Jesus Christ, and in the Spirit of our God."

From the very moment of belief in Jesus Christ's atoning work, the believer (being set apart) becomes a "saint" he is "holy" positionally.

1st Corinthians 1:2–3 "To the church of God which is at Corinth, to those who have been sanctified in Christ Jesus, saints by calling, with all who in every place call upon the name of our Lord Jesus Christ, their Lord and ours: Grace to you and peace from God our Father and the Lord Jesus Christ."

Hebrews 3:1 "Therefore, holy brethren, partakers of a heavenly calling, consider Jesus, the Apostle and High Priest of our confession."

The *second* time or period of sanctification is progressive. It is the practical time of sanctification that occurs in a progressive manner as the believer becomes more and more dedicated. He begins to progress in sanctification, as he dies daily to sin. Living his life separated unto God, and allowing himself to be lead and taught by the Holy Spirit, he remains in fellowship and service, and he seeks to become more conformed to the image of Christ.

Romans 6:5–11 "For if we have become united with Him in the likeness of His death, certainly we shall be also in the likeness of His resurrection, knowing this, that our old self was crucified with Him, that our body of sin might be done away with, that we should no longer be slaves to sin; for he who has died is freed from sin. Now if we have died with Christ, we believe that we shall also live with Him, knowing that Christ, having been raised from the dead, is never to die again; death no longer is master over Him. For the death that He died, He died to sin, once for all; but the life that He lives, He lives to God. Even so consider yourselves to be dead to sin, but alive to God in Christ Jesus."

John 17:17 "Sanctify them in the truth; Thy word is truth."

The Greek word "hagiamos," used in the New Testament means "holy" (holiness, sanctification, sanctified) signifies being "set apart for God" (hagiazo).

The *third* phase of sanctification is final. This will occur at the Second Coming of Christ.

1st Thessalonians 3:12–13 "And may the Lord cause you to increase and abound in love for one another, and for all men, just as we also do for you; so that He may establish your hearts unblamable in holiness before our God and Father at the coming of our Lord Jesus with all His saints."

1st John 3:2 "Beloved, now we are children of God, and it has not appeared as yet what we shall be. We know that, when He appears, we shall be like Him, because we shall see Him just as He is."

Human involvement is also required. To be sanctified one must:

Sanctification involves God the Blood of Jesus, The Holy Spirit, and the Word . . . Divine elements.

Have Faith in the Atonement

Hebrews 10:10 "By this will we have been sanctified through the offering of the body of Jesus Christ once for all."

Be Obedient to the Word of God

John 15:3 "You are already clean because of the word which I have spoken to you."

Show Humility

Romans 6:19 "I am speaking in human terms because of the weakness of your flesh. For just as you presented your members as slaves to impurity and to lawlessness, resulting in further lawlessness, so now present your members as slaves to righteousness, resulting in sanctification." ❖

NOTES

NOTES

PNEUMATOLOGY: THE DOCTRINE OF THE HOLY SPIRIT

The word "Pneuma" is Greek meaning, spirit, wind or breath.

Pneumatology is the doctrine of the ***spirit*** or ***breath*** of God, The Holy Spirit. This doctrine is of the Christian religion only.

It is an error to refer to The Holy Spirit as "it." This error is mainly due to the invisibility of the Spirit. Because He is not seen as having a body or shape, ascribing a personality to Him is difficult for some. The Holy Spirit is an invisible person . . . He is a personality.

The gifts of the Holy Spirit are distinguished from His personality. 1st Corinthians 12:1–14

THE HOLY SPIRIT AS A PERSONALITY POSSESSES THE FOLLOWING:

Intelligence

Isaiah 11:2 "And the Spirit of the LORD will rest on Him, the spirit of wisdom and understanding, the spirit of counsel and strength, the spirit of knowledge and the fear of the LORD."

A Will

1st Corinthians 12:11 "But one and the same Spirit works all these things, distributing to each one individually just as He wills."

A Mind

Romans 8:27 "And He who searches the hearts knows what the mind of the Spirit is, because He intercedes for the saints according to the will of God."

Feelings

Ephesians 4:30 "And do not grieve the Holy Spirit of God, by whom you were sealed for the day of redemption."

Power

Romans 15:13 "Now may the God of hope fill you with all joy and peace in believing, that you may abound in hope by the power of the Holy Spirit."

ACTIVITIES OF THE HOLY SPIRIT

He Reveals

2nd Peter 1:21 "For no prophecy was ever made by an act of human will, but men moved by the Holy Spirit spoke from God."

He Teaches

John 14:26 "But the Helper, the Holy Spirit, whom the Father will send in My name, He will teach you all things, and bring to your remembrance all that I said to you."

He Intercedes

Romans 8:26 "And in the same way the Spirit also helps our weakness; for we do not know how to pray as we should, but the Spirit Himself intercedes for us with groanings too deep for words."

He Commands

Acts 16:6–7 "And they passed through the Phrygian and Galatian region, having been forbidden by the Holy Spirit to speak the word in Asia; and when they had come to Mysia, they were trying to go into Bithynia, and the Spirit of Jesus did not permit them."

He Speaks

Revelation 2:7 "He who has an ear, let him hear what the Spirit says to the churches. To him who overcomes, I will grant to eat of the tree of life, which is in the Paradise of God."

He Endues with Power

Acts 1:8 "But you shall receive power when the Holy Spirit has come upon you; and you shall be My witnesses both in Jerusalem, and in all Judea and Samaria, and even to the remotest part of the earth."

He Bestows Supernatural Gifts

1st Corinthians 12:7–10 "But to each one is given the manifestation of the Spirit for the common good. For to one is given the word of wisdom through the Spirit, and to another the Word of knowledge according to the same Spirit; to another faith by the same Spirit, and to another gifts of healing by the one Spirit, and to another the effecting of miracles, and to another prophecy, and to another the distinguishing of spirits, to another various kinds of tongues, and to another the interpretation of tongues."

The Gifts of the Spirit

Word of Wisdom:
(utterance of wisdom)

Word of Knowledge:
(supernatural knowledge)

Faith:
(spiritual faith)

Healings:
(gifts given by God)

Miracles:
(John 14:12)

Prophecy:
(words that edify the body)

Discernment:
(distinguishing spirits)

Tongues:
(speaking a supernatural language)

Interpretation of Tongues:
(translation of supernatural languages)

Divine Attributes of the Holy Spirit

Divine attributes are also ascribed to the Holy Spirit as is to God the Father and God the Son.

The Holy Spirit is:

Eternal

Hebrews 9:14 "How much more will the blood of Christ, who through the eternal Spirit offered Himself without blemish to God, cleanse your conscience from dead works to serve the living God?"

Omnipotent

Luke 1:35 "And the angel answered and said to her, 'The Holy Spirit will come upon you, and the power of the Most High will overshadow you; and for that reason the holy offspring shall be called the Son of God'"

Omnipresent

Psalm 139:7–10 "Where can I go from Thy Spirit? Or where can I flee from Thy presence? If I ascend to heaven, Thou art there; If I make my bed in Sheol, behold, Thou art there. If I take the wings of the dawn, If I dwell in the remotest part of the sea, Even there Thy hand will lead me, And Thy right hand will lay hold of me."

Omniscient

1st Corinthians 2:10–11 "For to us God revealed them through the Spirit; for the Spirit searches all things, even the depths of God. For who among men knows the thoughts of a man except the spirit of the man, which is in him? Even so the thoughts of God no one knows except the Spirit of God."

The Holy Spirit is the 3rd person of the Godhead. He is the administrator of the Godhead.

The Work of the Holy Spirit

The Holy Spirit works in the physical sphere as well as the moral sphere. For instance:

In Creation

Genesis 1:2 "And the earth was formless and void, and darkness was over the surface of the deep; and the Spirit of God was moving over the surface of the water."

In Regeneration

John 3:5–8 "Jesus answered, 'Truly, truly, I say to you, unless one is born of water and the Spirit, he cannot enter into the kingdom of God. That which is born of the flesh is flesh, and that which is born of the Spirit is spirit. Do not marvel that I said to you, You must be born again. The wind blows where it wishes and you hear the sound of it, but do not know where it comes from and where it is going; so is everyone who is born of the Spirit.'"

In Resurrection

Romans 8:11 "But if the Spirit of Him who raised Jesus from the dead dwells in you, He who raised Christ Jesus from the dead will also give life to your mortal bodies through His Spirit who indwells you."

In Salvation

1st Corinthians 6:11 "And such were some of you; but you were washed, but you were sanctified, but you were justified in the name of the Lord Jesus Christ, and in the Spirit of our God."

In the World [67]

John 16:7–8 "But I tell you the truth, it is to your advantage that I go away; for if I do not go away, the Helper shall not come to you; but if I go, I will send Him to you. And He when He comes will convict the world concerning sin, and righteousness, and judgment; concerning sin, because they do not believe in Me."

[67] The Holy Spirit convicts the unbeliever.

Names of the Holy Spirit

The Spirit of God [68]

Matthew 28:19 "Go therefore and make disciples of all the nations, baptizing them in the name of the Father and the Son and the Holy Spirit."

The Spirit of Christ [69]

John 16:14 "He shall glorify Me; for He shall take of Mine, and shall disclose it to you."

Christ baptizes the believer in the Holy Spirit so that the "new life" can be retained.

[68] The Holy Spirit is absolutely Divine in every sense. He is God the Holy Spirit and is therefore recognized with God the Father and God the Son. Because of His Divinity, He is called the Spirit of God.

[69] He was sent by Christ, He came in the name of Christ and His special mission is to glorify Christ.

Romans 8:9 "However, you are not in the flesh but in the Spirit, if indeed the Spirit of God dwells in you. But if anyone does not have the Spirit of Christ, he does not belong to Him."

The Comforter [70]

John 14:16 "I will pray the Father and He shall give you another Comforter, that He may abide in you forever." (King James Version)

The Holy Spirit is our Promise [71]

The Old Testament Promise of the Spirit

Ezekiel 36:27 "And I will put my Spirit within you and cause you to walk in my statutes."

New Testament Promise of the Spirit

Luke 24:49 "Behold I send the promise of My Father upon you."

The Spirit of Truth [72]

Christ's mission was to reveal the Father. The Holy Spirit's mission, is to reveal the Son.

John 16:13 "But when He, the Spirit of truth, comes, He will guide you into all truth; for He will not speak on His own initiative, but whatever He hears, He will speak; and He will disclose to you what is to come."

The Spirit of Grace [73]

Hebrews 10:29 "How much severer punishment do you think he will deserve who has trampled under foot the Son of God, and has regarded as unclean the blood of the covenant by which he was sanctified, and has insulted the Spirit of grace?"

The Spirit of Life

Romans 8:2 "For the law of the Spirit of life in Christ Jesus has set you free from the law of sin and of death."

The Spirit of Adoption

Romans 8:15 "For you have not received a spirit of slavery leading to fear again, but you have received a spirit of adoption as sons by which we cry out, 'Abba! Father!'"

The Holy Spirit is who reveals the ***"Glorified Christ"*** in the Church. It is by the Holy Spirit that the omnipresence of Christ is made possible in the world.

[70] Comforter: Study John Chapters 14–17

[71] The disciples were promised another comforter, helper and teacher. Comforter in Greek is ***"Paracletos."*** A "paracletos" was one who stood by in danger, difficulties and trial.

The Latin word ***"advocate"*** was one who gave advice on what to do, what to say and in times, he himself spoke on behalf of the person. The "advocate" was the comforter that gave of himself not for hire, but out of love and concern.

[72] He speaks to us to further reveal the words of Jesus and of what He hears within the life of the Godhead.

[73] The Holy Spirit strives with man for the betterment of his soul. He gives man the grace to repent. 1st Peter 1:10–13

Romans 9:4
Ephesians 1:5

Symbols of the Holy Spirit

God has given us symbols as illustrations, which describe some of the operations of the Holy Spirit.

Oil

Hebrews 1:9 "Thou has loved righteousness and hated lawlessness; Therefore God, Thy God, hath anointed Thee with the Oil of Gladness above Thy companions."

Water

John 7:38 "He who believes in Me, as the Scripture said, 'From his innermost being shall flow rivers of living water.'"

Wind

Acts 2:2 "And suddenly there came from heaven a noise like a violent, rushing wind, and it filled the whole house where they were sitting."

Fire

Acts 2:3 "And there appeared to them tongues as of fire distributing themselves, and they rested on each one of them."

A Dove

Matthew 3:16 "And after being baptized, Jesus went up immediately from the water; and behold, the heavens were opened, and He saw the Spirit of God descending as a dove, and coming upon Him."

A Seal

Ephesians 1:13 "In Him, you also, after listening to the message of truth, the gospel of your salvation—having believed, you were sealed in Him with the Holy Spirit of promise."

Sins against the Holy Spirit

Grieving the Holy Spirit

Ephesians 4:30 "And do not grieve the Holy Spirit of God, by whom you were sealed from the day of redemption."

Vexing the Holy Spirit

Isaiah 63:10 "But they rebelled and grieved His Holy Spirit; therefore, He turned Himself to become their enemy, He fought against them."

Resisting the Holy Spirit

Acts 7:51 "You men are stiff-necked and uncircumcised in heart and ears are always resisting the Holy Spirit; you are doing just as your fathers did."

Blaspheming the Holy Spirit

Mark 3:29–30 "But whoever blasphemes against the Holy Spirit never has forgiveness, but is guilty of an eternal sin because they were saying, 'He has an unclean spirit.'"

Lying to the Holy Spirit

Acts 5:3 "But Peter said, 'Ananias, why has Satan filled your heart to lie to the Holy Spirit, and to keep back some of the price of the land?'"

Quenching the Holy Spirit [74]

1st Thessalonians 5:19 "Do not quench the Spirit." ❖

[74] Forbidding or withholding the gifts of the Holy Spirit to be in operation.

NOTES

NOTES

THE DOCTRINE OF SCRIPTURE

It took approximately twenty centuries and nearly forty-four inspired writers to produce one of the greatest pieces of literature this world has ever known . . . **The Bible.** The Bible is one great compilation of books. Its truths, testaments and single theme is discoursed throughout all of its sixty-six books in harmony and in unity. Within its pages is the witness of the revelation and acts of "one God" and His relationship with humanity. As the Holy Spirit moved upon men, the compelling truth was unfolded giving us (in a progressive manner) one great affirmation of redemption—the person and work of Jesus Christ.

WHAT ARE THE SCRIPTURES?

God's desire is to maintain spiritual communion with man. This is not hard to conceive because man was made in the image and likeness of God, and is therefore able to communicate with Him. Adam, who talked with God on a daily basis, is our first example. Unfortunately, the fall of Adam and Eve resulted in alternative modes of conversing between God and man.

Of all the variations of communication between God and man, one stands unique above all ... God's written Word. The word "Bible" is derived from the Greek word "Biblios" which means "Book." The Bible consists of sixty–six divinely inspired volumes that are divided into two sections, which relate to two divine Covenants: (The Old Testament—The Covenant of Law and The New Testament—The Covenant of Grace).

OTHER NAMES FOR THE WORD OF GOD

The Law [75]

Psalm 19:7 "The law of the LORD is perfect, restoring the soul."

Statutes

Psalm 19:8 "The precepts of the LORD are right, rejoicing the heart."

Commandments

Psalm 19:8 "The commandment of the LORD is pure, enlightening the eyes."

[75a] The Law of God is Perfect. Psalm. 119–142, Romans 7:12, 1st Timothy 1:8

[75b] The Law is Perpetual. Leviticus 23:14

[75c] The Law is Impartial. Leviticus 24:22

Deuteronomy 4:1
Psalm 119:112

Psalm 119:6
Matthew 15:3

Truth

2nd Samuel 7:28 "And now, O Lord GOD, Thou art God, and Thy words are truth, and Thou hast promised this good thing to Thy servant."

Psalm 146:6
Psalm 33:4

The Scriptures

Matthew 22:29 "But Jesus answered and said to them, 'You are mistaken, not understanding the Scriptures, or the power of God.'"

John 5:39
1st Corinthians 15:3

Holy Scriptures

Romans 1:2 "Which He promised beforehand through His prophets in the Holy Scriptures."

2nd Timothy 3:5

The Book of the LORD

Isaiah 34:16 "See from the book of the LORD, and read."

The Word

James 1:21–23 "Therefore putting aside all filthiness and all that remains of wickedness, in humility receive the word implanted, which is able to save your souls. But prove yourselves doers of the word, and not merely hearers who delude themselves. For if anyone is a hearer of the word and not a doer, he is like a man who looks at his natural face in a mirror."

Oracles of God

Romans 3:2 "Great in every respect. First of all, that they were entrusted with the oracles of God."

1st Peter 4:11

The Word of Christ

Colossians 3:16 "Let the word of Christ richly dwell within you, with all wisdom teaching and admonishing one another with psalms and hymns and spiritual songs, singing with thankfulness in your hearts to God."

The Word of Life

1st John 1:1 "What was from the beginning, what we have heard, what we have seen with our eyes, what we beheld and our hand handled, concerning the Word of Life."

Philippians 2:16

The Word of Truth

2nd Timothy 2:15 "Be diligent to present yourself

James 1:18

approved to God as a workman who does not need to be ashamed, handling accurately the word of truth."

The Word of God

Revelation 19:13 "And He is clothed with a robe dipped in blood; and His name is called The Word of God."

The Word of the Cross

1st Corinthians 1:18 "For the word of the cross is to those who are perishing foolishness, but to us who are being saved it is the power of God."

The Sword of the Spirit

Ephesians 6:17 "And take The Helmet of Salvation, and the sword of the Spirit, which is the word of God."

The Writings of Truth

Daniel 10:21a "However, I will tell you what is inscribed in the writing of truth."

"Book"

Revelation 22:19

Psalm 40:7 "Then I said, 'Behold, I come; In the scroll of the book it is written of me.'"

The Word of Faith

Romans 10:8 "But what does it say? 'The Word is near you, in your mouth and in your heart.'—that is, the word of faith which we are preaching."

Use of the Word of God

God's Word was given to man for many beneficial reasons. However, man has a responsibility to not only take heed but to practice God's Word so as to discover its divine intent. Therefore, the Word of God should be:

Studied Daily

Acts 17:11

Nehemiah 8:18 "And he read from the book of the law of God daily, from the first day to the last day. And they celebrated the feast seven days, and on the eighth day there was a solemn assembly according to the ordinance."

Read in Public

Colossians 4:16
Nehemiah 8:3
2nd Kings 23:2

Luke 4:16 "And He came to Nazareth, where He had

been brought up; and as was His custom, He entered the synagogue on the Sabbath, and stood up to read."

Spoken

***Titus* 2:15** "These things speak and exhort and reprove with all authority. Let no one disregard you."

***Acts* 5:20**
***Ezekiel* 2:7**
***Jeremiah* 1:7**

Kept

***John* 14:23** "Jesus answered and said to him, 'If anyone loves Me, he will keep My word; and My Father will love him, and We will come to him, and make Our abode with him.'"

***John* 8:51**
***Proverbs* 28:7**

Performed

***James* 1:22** "But prove yourselves doers of the word, and not merely hearers who delude themselves."

The Nature of the Written Word of God is:

Sacred [76]

***Deuteronomy* 12:32** "Whatever I command you, you shall be careful to do; you shall not add to nor take away from it."

[76] God's Word should not be tampered with. Romans 7:14, Revelation 22:19

Profitable for *instruction, knowledge* and *blessings*

***Luke* 24:32** "And they said to one another, 'Were not our hearts burning within us while He was speaking to us on the road, while He was explaining the Scriptures to us?'"

***Matthew* 22:29** "But Jesus answered and said to them, 'You are mistaken, not understanding the Scriptures, or the power of God.'"

***Revelation* 1:3** "Blessed is he who reads and those who hear the words of the prophecy, and heed the things which are written in it; for the time is near."

***Luke* 11:28**

Realistic of life's experiences [77]

1st *Corinthians* 10:11 "Now these things happened to them as an example, and they were written for our instruction, upon whom the ends of the ages have come."

[77] God's Word was written giving real life experiences to use as examples.

***Psalm* 119:11**

Purposeful [78]

***John* 20:31** "But these have been written that you may believe that Jesus is the Christ, the Son of God;

[78] It not only reveals God's plan and purpose for His people, it also assists in building faith in Christ and a more spiritual life.

and that believing you may have life in His name."

Foundational [79]

James 1:18 "In the exercise of His will He brought us forth by the word of truth, so that we might be, as it were, the first fruits among His creatures."

[79] The Word of God sets the standards of Christian faith for the believer and the church.

1st Thessalonians 2:13

Ageless, it is forever established

Mark 13:31 "Heaven and earth will pass away, but My words will not pass away."

Psalm 119:89

Pure [80]

Psalm 19:8 "The precepts of the LORD are right, rejoicing the heart; The commandment of the LORD is pure, enlightening the eyes."

[80] The Word of God is unadulterated and undefiled.

Absolute, it is sure

Psalm 111:7 "The works of His hands are truth and justice; All His precepts are sure."

Psalm 93:5
Isaiah 40:8
1st Kings 8:56

Characteristically God's Written Word:

Heals

Matthew 8:8 "But the centurion answered and said, 'Lord, I am not worthy for You to come under my roof, but just say the word, and my servant will be healed.'"

Matthew 24:35
Matthew 5:18

Endures

1st Peter 1:25 "But the word of the LORD abides forever. And, this is the word which was preached to you."

Abides

1st Peter 1:23 "For you have been born again not of seed which is perishable but imperishable, that is, through the living and abiding word of God."

Sanctifies

1st Timothy 4:4–5 "For everything created by God is good, and nothing is to be rejected, if it is received with gratitude; for it is sanctified by means of the word of God and prayer."

Ephesians 5:26
Colossians 1:22

Saves

Romans 1:16 "For I am not ashamed of the gospel, for it is the power of God for salvation to everyone who believes, to the Jew first and also the Greek."

Purifies

Psalm 119:9 "How can a young man keep his way pure? By keeping it according to Thy word."

God's written Word gives:

Success

Joshua 1:8 "This book of the law shall not depart from your mouth, but you shall meditate on it day and night, so that you may be careful to do according to all that is written in it; for then you will make your way prosperous, and then you will have success."

Warnings

1st Corinthians 10:11 "Now these things happened to them as an example, and they were written for our instruction, upon whom the ends of the ages have come."

Light

Psalm 119:130 "The unfolding of Thy words gives light; It gives understanding to the simple."

Life

Ezekiel 37:7 "So I prophesied as I was commanded; and as I prophesied, there was a noise, and behold, a rattling; and the bones came together, bone to its bone."

Hope

Romans 15:4 "For whatever was written in earlier times was written for our instruction, that through perseverance and the encouragement of the Scriptures we might have hope."

The Word of God is:

A Weapon

Ephesians 6:17 "And take the Helmet of Salvation, and the sword of the Spirit, which is the word of God."

Sharp

Hebrews 4:12 "For the word of God is living and active and sharper than any two–edged sword, and piercing as far as the division of soul and spirit, of both joints and marrow, and able to judge the thoughts and intentions of the heart."

Prophetic

2nd Peter 1:19 "And so we have the prophetic word made more sure, to which you do well to pay attention as to a lamp shining in a dark place, until the day dawns and the morning star arises in your hearts."

Sweet

Psalm 119:103 "How sweet are Thy words to my taste! Yes, sweeter than honey to my mouth!"

A Lamp

Proverbs 6:23 "For the commandment is a lamp, and the teaching is light; And reproofs for discipline are the way of life."

Faithful

Titus 1:9 "Holding fast the faithful word which is in accordance with the teaching, that he may be able both to exhort in sound doctrine and to refute those who contradict."

Good

Hebrews 6:5 "And have tasted the good word of God and the powers of the age to come."

Living

Hebrews 4:12a "For the word of God is living and active and sharper than any two–edged sword."

God's Word is also like:

Food

Job 23:12 "I have not departed from the command of His lips; I have treasured the words of His mouth more than my necessary food."

Milk

1st Peter 2:2 "Like newborn babes, long for the pure milk of the word, that by it you may grow in respect to salvation."

A Seed

Mark 4:14 "The sower sows the word."

A Flame

Jeremiah 5:14 "Therefore, thus says the LORD, the God of hosts, 'Because you have spoken this word, Behold, I am making My words in your mouth fire and this people wood, and it will consume them.'"

A Hammer

Jeremiah 23:29 "'Is not My word like fire?' declares the LORD, 'and like a hammer which shatters a rock?'"

And, His people love God's Word

Psalm 119:92 "If Thy law had not been my delight, Then I would have perished in my affliction."

Jeremiah 15:16 "Thy words were found and I ate them, And Thy words became for me a joy and the delight of my heart; For I have been called by Thy name, O LORD God of hosts."

The Source of God's Word

There are three divine processes that are involved in the written Word of God. They are *revelation, inspiration* and *illumination.*

The Holy Spirit, who is the third person of the Godhead or Trinity, achieves all three making the Bible the only authoritative truth.

Revelation

Revelation means ***unveiling*** or ***disclosure***. This is the method used by God to reveal Himself and His plan for human life.

While disclosing or making Himself known, man is somewhat passive because he is receiving God's revelation and instructions pertaining to it.

Galatians 1:12 "For I neither received it from man, nor was I taught it, but I received it through a revelation of Jesus Christ." ***Deuteronomy 29:29***

Revelation 1:10–11 "I was in the Spirit on the Lord's day, and I heard behind me a loud voice like the sound of a trumpet, saying, 'Write in a book what you see, and send it to the seven churches: to Ephesus and to

Smyrna and to Pergamum and to Thyatira and to Sardis and to Philadelphia and to Laodicea.'"

Inspiration

Inspiration in Scripture means, "God–breathed." After disclosing Himself and making His will known, God breathed upon His servants so that they responded to the revelation. Coming out of a state of passivity, they became active in the process of writing the revelation.

Revelation 1:11
Exodus 17:14
2nd Timothy 3:15–17

2nd Timothy 3:15–17 "And that from childhood you have known the sacred writings which are able to give you the wisdom that leads to salvation through faith which is in Christ Jesus. All Scripture is inspired by God and profitable for teaching, for reproof, for correction, for training in righteousness; that the man of God may be adequate, equipped for every good work."

2nd Peter 1:20–21 "But know this first of all, that no prophecy of Scripture is a matter of one's own interpretation, for no prophecy was ever made by an act of human will, but men moved by the Holy Spirit spoke from God."

Illumination

The *revelation* and *inspirational* process of the written Word of God has already been achieved and cannot be changed. The third process, is however, a continual one. Illumination is what God gives to the mind of the reader so that it can be understood. In essence, God sheds light on His Word. He makes the truth and authority of it comprehensible. Therefore, the illumination of the Word is divine.

Mark 13:31
John 16:12–15
Acts 17:1–3

Luke 24:45 "Then He opened their minds to understand the Scriptures."

Because the source of God's written Word is divine and is not conceived or bought into existence by the human mind or imagination, it is authentic, authoritative, infallible and everlasting. ❖

1st John 2:25–27

NOTES

NOTES

CHAPTER 1 SUMMARY

BIBLE DOCTRINE

Doctrine is also called ***theology***, which means discourse about God. Both terms are sciences that deal primarily with the knowledge of God and God's relationship with man. It also contributes to the zeal of witnessing and propagation of God's Word.

THEOLOGY—The Doctrine of God

The Bible does not prove the existence of God; rather it makes "affirmation" of His existence.

Knowing the various names by which God is called is helpful in building a relationship with Him. Of the names He is called, **"Yahweh"** (which is the name He called Himself) should not be used by anyone else.

The name Jehovah is compounded with descriptions of God's involvement with His people.

The attributes of God help us relate to Him. The three categories of His attributes are:

1) Who God is apart from man
2) What God is to the universe
3) God's relationship with His moral beings

Careful consideration must be taken to avoid confusing the names of God with His attributes.

Questions:

1. What proof do we have of the existence of God?
2. What is meant by "cosmological" proof?
3. Explain the "effect" of the universe?
4. What is meant by "teleological" proof?
5. Can any human prove the existence of God? Give the reason for your answer.
6. List the names of God and give definitions.
7. Describe the false views of God.

Practical Application

You are in a conversation with someone who does not believe in God. This person is in a situation that has him feeling depressed . . . he feels hopeless. He also feels as if life is passing him by and he has experienced some awful things and would say to you "there cannot be a God if life is the way it is." How would you use what you have learned to convince this person that God does exist?

CHAPTER 2 SUMMARY

ANGELOLOGY—The Doctrine of Angels

Angels are celestial creatures that were created by God and who are agents that perform special assignments for Him. They have several characteristics and attributes which make them somewhat superior to man. Angels are described in categories and are ranked in Scripture. There are holy angels as well as fallen angels (who are chained in hell awaiting judgement), and there are evil angels. These angels are also referred to as Satan's angels, fallen angels, wicked spirits or demons, seductive spirits, unclean spirits and they dwell in the world. The names of these spirits help to identify their activities.

Questions:

1. What are the characteristics of angels?
2. What is a Theophany?
3. What classification of angel is Michael?
4. What is the work of Cherubims?
5. Name the attributes of angels.
6. Find the passages of Scripture that describes Satan's expulsion from heaven.
7. List some of the characteristics of Satan's angels.
8. Why do you think Satan is called the "god" of this age?
9. Read Ezekiel 28:14–15; 28:12–17 and Isaiah 14:12–15. Give the original position of Satan, what his name meant and the cause of his downfall.
10. What are some of the activities of Satan?

CHAPTER 3 SUMMARY

HAMARTIOLOGY—THE DOCTRINE OF SIN

God created all things except sin. God being righteous and having no faults, would not contradict His own nature or His morality. Man has been given a will of his own to use freely. He makes choices that are either right or wrong. The conscience of man helps him to identify the difference between the two. The Bible gives a clear explanation of this and the entrance of sin into the human race that is embedded in the nature of man. Sin is clearly an action that is taken with the knowledge of its opposition to the will of God and its subsequent consequences.

QUESTIONS:

1. How did Satan introduce sin into the human race?
2. The reality of sin is declared in what three ways?
3. Identify the "nature" of the following sins:
   - Sinners miss the divine aim of God.
   - Over stepping the Law or divine boundaries between good and evil.
   - The departure from right by way of ignorance. *Hebrews 9:7*
   - The intrusion of self–will into the sphere of divine authority. *Ephesians 2:1*
   - To be without worship or reverence. *Romans 1:18*
   - The sinner who makes a god of self, breaking the commandments of God and keeping his own. *1st John 3:4*
4. What are the three deaths described in Scripture?
5. Explain "destruction" as a penalty of sin.

CHAPTER 4 SUMMARY

CHRISTOLOGY—The Doctrine of Christ

The virgin birth of Christ gives the basis for the doctrine of incarnation; God became man . . . "The Son of God." This does not imply that God ceased to be God. Rather, it proves the power of God and His love for man (which is described in His attributes). Christ (also known as the Messiah) provided Himself as the "sacrifice of all sacrifices" for sin (as seen in His redemptive work). He showed Himself as an example of righteousness and perfection for man to follow and strive for in this life. He, being the Word or Logos, also promises man eternal life with Him (the Way Preparer). In order to achieve this for mankind, He identified Himself with man's infirmities and weaknesses by naming Himself "Son of Man," which depicts His faithfulness to His mission and affection for those who would believe.

God manifested in the flesh was precisely planned to regain the fellowship that was lost because of sin. The types of atonement (which foreshadowed Christ the "once and for all" sacrifice) became redundant and proved incapable of appeasing the offenses made toward God. Christ fulfilled the requirements for divine restitution for sin.

Christ held three offices as the mediator between God and His People. He was the perfect prophet, priest and king. Yet, the most significant work of Christ was His dying for man's sins . . . this accomplished atonement. Through His resurrection, Christ proved His claims of being a Savior.

Questions:

1. Give the reason why "Son of God" proclaims Deity.
2. Jesus is called "Son of Man." Give three explanations of this title.
3. Describe the basis of the doctrine of incarnation.
4. Why is Jesus called "the Word?"

Practical Application

You are talking with someone who wants to understand how God became man and why. This person also wants you to explain how he can start his life over again. He is with his wife who is a very nice person, and believes that being a good person is enough to get into heaven. She believes that doing good deeds will cause God to forget about your sins, because after all God is merciful. They are both very anxious people who talk fast and leave little or no room for long explanations. How would you explain Christ, which of the names of Christ would you use to briefly explain that He is The Son of God? And, how would you explain the reason for Christ's death?

CHAPTER 5 SUMMARY

SOTERIOLOGY—The Doctrine of Salvation

The quest of being in fellowship or in right standing with God is experienced by everyone at some time in their life, even if it's denied. All efforts become futile when the atoning work of Jesus Christ is denied or ignored. God's grace to forgive man's sins is not based on what a man does, nor is it simply a favorable act of God. God is the righteous judge of sin and to be absolved one must accept His righteous provision. Forgiveness of sin and its penalty is gained through the redemptive and propitiatory work of Jesus Christ. This is the only means by which justification can be obtained.

The struggle between the two natures is continual. However, the re–birth of man's nature (regeneration) gives him the power to subdue what he is prone to . . . sin. Regeneration is in contrast to reformation because it is an action undertaken by God and not man's self will.

Sanctification and holiness (being set apart for God) means living a life that perpetuates righteousness with the assistance of the Holy Spirit. The believer remains in fellowship and service with God and seeks to be more conformed to the image of Christ. The divine elements involved in living a sanctified life is God, the blood of Jesus, the help of the Holy Spirit and obedience to God's Word.

Questions:

1. What are the three aspects of salvation?
2. Briefly explain justification.
3. Find three Scriptures that support the fact that a price was paid for man's redemption.
4. Explain the three phases of sanctification.
5. What is man's involvement in sanctification?
6. Explain the four divine elements involved in sanctification.

Practical Application

A young man gives his life to the Lord. He desperately wants to overcome the bad habit of smoking, and he comes to you for assistance. His mind is filled with the idea that he cannot really be saved and sanctified unto God. He's heard many sermons about sinners in the church and feels he is a hypocrite that God has no use for. How would you explain salvation to him using what you have learned about justification, regeneration and sanctification to encourage him to continue his walk with the Lord?

CHAPTER 6 SUMMARY

PNEUMATOLOGY—The Doctrine of the Holy Spirit

The word "Pneuma" is Greek for spirit, wind or breath. The Holy Spirit is not an "it" or a "thing" as some may refer to Him. The Holy Spirit is absolutely divine in every sense. He is God the Holy Spirit and is therefore recognized with God the Father and God the Son. Because of His Divinity, He is called the Spirit of God. He is the Third Person of the Godhead or Trinity and a person (God). He has a personality, and being the Spirit of God, the Holy Spirit possesses the same divine attributes as God the Father.

Several names and symbols in Scripture describe the Holy Spirit and help us to understand His functions. His mission is two-fold:

(1) Being sent by Christ and coming in the name of Christ, His primary mission is to glorify Christ Jesus in the Church and reveal Him to the world. The Holy Spirit strives with man for the betterment of his soul.

(2) He dwells in the believer to assist him in his walk with Christ. He is an intercessor, advocate, paracletos and comforter.

Questions:

1. Why is it difficult for some to relate to the Holy Spirit as a person?
2. What are the characteristics of the Holy Spirit that define Him as a person?
3. What is the Holy Spirit's involvement in the Trinity?
4. Why is it an error to refer to the Holy Spirit as an "it" or "thing?"
5. Why is the Holy Spirit called "The Spirit of God?"
6. List five activities of the Holy Spirit.
7. What are the names of the Holy Spirit?
8. Explain "blasphemy" against the Holy Spirit.
9. What does quenching the Holy Spirit mean?
10. How can you grieve the Holy Spirit?
11. Define the Latin word "advocate."
12. What is the Greek word for "comforter?"
13. The Holy Spirit is called the Spirit of Christ. Explain why.

CHAPTER 7 SUMMARY

THE DOCTRINE OF SCRIPTURE

God has always communicated with man in various ways. However, the most unique way of all is His written Word . . . The Bible.

God's Word was given to man for reasons that are beneficial for standards of faith and living a life that is pleasing to Him. The Word of God contains real life experiences and stories of God's deliverance from calamities and the hardships of life. It unfolds the mystery of God's love and His plan to keep His most superior creation in fellowship with Him despite his sinfulness. The Bible gives awareness of the existence of God, but most of all, it demonstrates His provision of love that brings peace, joy and the hope of eternal life.

With its many definitions, mysteries, cryptic passages, and symbolism, the Bible is a magnificent book that should be read at least once in every man's lifetime. For in it is the revelation of God and how He relates to man. Being compiled by the divine methods of revelation, inspiration and illumination of the Holy Spirit, the Bible remains the only authoritative Word of God. In spite of the harshness of scrutiny, criticisms that set platforms for philosophical debates, and grounds for misinterpretation that provide the foundations for strange and bizarre practices of faith with erroneous doctrines, God's written Word is infallible and everlasting. Man would do well to take heed to its truths and accept the blessings it contains while being cautious not to tamper with that which is holy and true.

QUESTIONS:

1. List ten Scriptures that relate to the Bible as the "Word of the Lord."
2. Find six Scriptures that describe the Bible as "The Word."
3. The Word of God is described as "pure." What does this mean?
4. Explain how the Scriptures are purposeful?
5. Find a passage of Scriptures that relates to one of your own life experiences.
6. Research the following Scriptures and give their description of the Word of God. *Colossians 3:16; Philippians 2:16; Ephesians 1:13; Romans 10:8*
7. Give the definitions of the following words relating to the Scriptures: Apocrypha, Authority, Inspiration, Oracle, Infallibility.

NOTES

NOTES

To preview the series
visit Judah Publications at:
www.judahpublications.com

In this series:

Volume 1: Introduction to Bible Doctrine
A Systematic Study of Seven Doctrines of the Christian Faith—Made Easy

Volume 2: Introduction to Bible Origin
A Study of the Formation of the Bible

Volume 3: Introduction to Typology and Symbolism
An Expository Study of Types and Symbols Found in the Bible

To receive credit toward a **Certificate in Bible Studies** for this series, send your request by:

e-mail:

ITMT@Bellsouth.net

or write:

The Institute of Theology and Ministry Training
P.O. Box 608505
Orlando, Florida 32860–8505